The Baby Sleep Plan

The
Baby
Sleep
Plan

Sleep Train Your Way to a Happy and Healthy Baby

REBECCA MICHI

ROCKRIDGE
PRESS

Interior and Cover Designer: Francesca Pacchini
Art Producer: Samantha Ulban
Editor: Emily Angell
Production Editor: Andrew Yackira

All images courtesy of © Shutterstock

ISBN: Print 978-1-64611-624-9 | eBook 978-1-64611-625-6

R0

To all the parents out there . . .
we're all in this together

Contents

Introduction

WELCOME! I AM SO GLAD YOU ARE HERE. Chances are you and your child are struggling with some sleep issues. Well, you have come to the right place. Let me start by telling you a little about me and how this book can help you and your baby get a better night's sleep.

I am a British-born children's sleep consultant. I gained my child-development qualification in England more than 25 years ago and have worked with many families in various capacities. I started working solely with children's sleep over a decade ago, and since then I have helped hundreds of families. Sleep isn't always as natural as we think it should be, and I want to make sleep as easy as possible for families. I look at a child's unique temperament as we begin to work toward a better night's sleep. The sleep-training techniques I use are gentle: A parent remains in the room and helps their child while they learn the skills to get themselves to sleep and back to sleep when they naturally wake up during the night.

If you search for "sleep training" on the internet, more than a million pages offering advice come up, and they often contradict one another. In fact, you can spend hours researching which technique to use and end up even more confused and frustrated, still not knowing which technique is best for your child or how to get started. In *The Baby Sleep Plan*, you'll learn about the main sleep-training techniques and how to implement them. You'll also learn how to figure out which method is best for your family.

The Baby Sleep Plan is straightforward and no-nonsense, giving you the tools you need to make positive changes. I share my favorite tips and tricks for making sleep training as easy as possible. We'll begin by looking at sleep and why it's so important, as well as how sleep changes as your child grows. Having an independent sleeper is not only beneficial to you but also great for your baby; they will have the skills to get to sleep at the beginning of the night as well as to get back to sleep when they wake during the night.

I'll help you identify your child's unique temperament to assist you in choosing a sleep-training technique that works for your child. This will get you off to the best possible start when sleep training because you won't be wasting time on a technique that won't work for your child. We'll look at how to work through the sleep training from start to finish and how to manage any bumps you may experience that could cause a setback. From travel to illness to exhaustion, you'll have the knowledge you need to work through it all. Throughout this book, you'll also find useful exercises, meditations, and journal prompts to help you pause and take a moment for yourself during this sleep-training journey. This book concludes with questions and answers that address some common, as well as not-so-common, sleep questions.

Remember, all babies are unique and develop differently, especially when it comes to sleep. Some children are sleeping through the night at 12 weeks, and some continue to need to feed during the night until they are nearly 12 months. There is no magical age, weight, or stage when a child no longer needs to feed during the night. Try not to compare your child against their siblings or your friends' children. You can certainly help them get the best possible sleep, but it may look very different from their peers.

I strongly suggest you speak with your child's pediatrician before you get started with sleep training. This book is not a substitute for medical advice; only your child's doctor can diagnose any possible medical issues that may be causing disruptions to their sleep. With that said, imagine how you'll feel when your child can get themselves to sleep at the beginning of the night, sleep for long stretches, get themselves back to sleep, and don't need to feed. How much better rested will you feel? How will your evenings be different?

Sleep training is not always easy, but it is always worth it. Without further ado, let's get started.

Chapter 1

The Lowdown on Sleep

FEW EVENTS ARE MORE EXCITING AND MORE terrifying than bringing a new baby home. We all know that babies sleep a lot, but you may not be sure just how much sleep they'll get or when they'll get it. New parents know that they're likely to be tired when they bring their baby home, but when will that stop? When will they sleep through the night? This chapter looks at what's "normal" when it comes to sleep and what you can expect. This sets the stage for the chapters that cover how to teach your child important skills to get themselves to sleep, as well as back to sleep when they wake up throughout the night.

The Importance of Sleep for Babies

We love sleep, and we know it's essential for all of us, but do you know why it is so important for your baby?

While your baby is sleeping, they are consolidating memories. Everything your child observed and learned during their short awake time is being filed away and stored while they are snoozing. Brain tissue is developing and growing, and connections between the left and right sides of the brain are made. These connections let the two sides of the brain talk to each other, and when these two sides are communicating, we have optimal thought processes. These thought processes are going to help your child as they grow as well as throughout their adult life. (By the way, Albert Einstein's genius is linked to well-connected brain hemispheres!)

Between your baby's birth and 12 weeks of age, their brain will almost double in volume. Growing 1 percent each day is tiring work; your child will need lots of calories and lots of sleep for such rapid development.

We all feel better after a good sleep. We make better food choices, we're less irritable, and we have an easier time sleeping. While your child doesn't have much choice when it comes to their food, better sleep will result in less irritability as well as an easier time feeding and napping. When we make sleep a priority, we are not only promoting brain development; we are also making awake periods more enjoyable for both you and your child.

You may think that the more tired your baby is, the easier time they will have sleeping, but the opposite is true: Overtired babies have a much harder time falling asleep and remaining asleep. Your child's brain can get overstimulated, and your little one may struggle to unwind. They may fight falling sleep, which can result in their needing much more help from you to get to sleep. They will also need more help remaining asleep (e.g., a lot more rocking and shushing).

Parents Need Sleep, Too!

Most adults need between seven and eight hours of sleep each night, and if we don't get that, we run the risk of being tired and, over the long term, becoming sleep deprived. Not only is nodding off during the day a real possibility (which you'll want to avoid when your child isn't napping), but sleep deprivation is linked to depression, memory lapses, irritability, increased blood pressure, diabetes, heart disease, and a whole host of other conditions. What's more, if you drive while sleep deprived, you are at risk of an accident; your reaction times are actually the same as if you were driving drunk! Even if you're not driving, your ability to respond to emergencies and your overall resilience to what the day throws at you can be severely impaired. Your body needs to sleep, and that's why you're learning to sleep train your child—not only for their well-being but yours, too.

Lack of Sleep versus Sleep Deprivation

A lack of sleep is a night or two of less sleep than you should get. For example, if you go to bed late and miss out on an hour of sleep for two nights, you're tired and lacking rest. If you miss out on an hour or more of sleep each night for a week, two weeks, a month, or longer, then you are sleep deprived. We can compensate for lack of sleep by sleeping in later or taking a nap, but we can't do that with sleep deprivation. That's why it's so important to get a good night's sleep consistently and take steps to improve your sleep if that's not happening.

EXERCISE: Nightly Self-Check

Often when we review our day, we think about things that didn't go well. That's understandable, but it's also important to think about the things that have gone well. Toward the end of each day, spend a few minutes going through this self-check on your own, share it with your partner, or write your responses in a journal.

○ **What has gone well today?** For example, "I took a walk with my baby and a friend. I managed to eat some lunch around lunchtime. I showered. I helped my baby nap for two hours."

○ **What didn't go so great today?** For example, "I felt so upset and cried when I couldn't get baby down for a nap. It rained all day, and we didn't get out for a walk. I think I'm getting a cold. The baby cried for what felt like hours and hours today."

○ **Is there anything I need help with?** For example, "If my partner made me some lunch when they made their own lunch in the morning, I would be able to eat earlier. I haven't showered in days. I'm going to shower when my mom comes over tomorrow, and she can hold the baby. I'm going to get a rain cover for the stroller, so I can get out and walk even if it is raining."

The Short- and Long-Term Effects of Sleep Issues

Isn't life easier when you feel well rested? The person who cut you off when you were driving to the store is not going to rattle you as much as when you are tired and cranky. You'll remember what you popped into the store for, where you put the car keys, and what you're looking for in the fridge. When you are well rested, you make better judgment calls and it's easier to focus. The opposite is true when you aren't getting adequate sleep, even in the short term.

If your child's night wakings are causing you to have disturbed sleep night after night, you may experience adverse health effects in addition to simply feeling tired. When you're tired, your immune system doesn't function as well, and your body will have a tougher time fighting off infection. What's more, blood pressure lowers during sleep, giving your heart and blood vessels the chance to rest, which lowers the risk of stroke and heart disease. Also, blood sugar levels reduce during sleep, which is necessary for avoiding health issues like diabetes, kidney disease, eye problems, and nerve damage. With sleep deprivation that's not addressed, these health issues are a real concern, but don't worry: Having a baby who disrupts your sleep for only a while won't cause you a never-ending stream of health problems. You'll start sleeping better soon! After all, that's why you picked up this book.

Fortunately, infants and babies are relatively good at managing their sleep; it is unusual for them to become sleep deprived. They can undoubtedly become tired and even overtired, which will impact their mood. They may be more irritable and crankier, have trouble feeding, and you may find that you struggle to wake them, which you may want to do to feed them. As children grow, if they do not get enough sleep on a regular basis and become sleep deprived, they will struggle a little more than when they were infants. You will continue to see irritability and crankiness, but now your child may have difficulty in school. They may have a harder time remembering things, which will undoubtedly make learning harder. Children can concentrate for longer and have better problem-solving abilities when better rested. Not only is schoolwork easier, but they also make better choices and don't take as many risks when they are sleeping well.

Physical Responses to Lack of Sleep

When your body is deprived of sleep for a prolonged period of time (that is, more than a few nights), the physical responses are apparent. You'll yawn more, your body will feel sluggish and heavy, and you'll notice darker circles under your eyes. Your hair might lose its shine, and your skin can become dry or break out in response. You're more likely to crave processed food for the quick sugar rush and to drink more coffee than usual, which can result in weight gain and an increase in the symptoms described.

For a child, they will struggle to fall asleep and remain asleep when they are overtired. You will need to help them much more, and any hopes of their getting themselves to sleep may be dashed.

Mental Responses to Lack of Sleep

When you haven't had enough sleep, you have a much harder time remembering things and recalling details. You'll struggle to focus and retain new information. When the brain doesn't have enough time asleep, it's not getting a chance to store away new memories. Your mind will feel foggy and it's likely to work at a much slower pace. It's the same for your child. Remember, while a baby is sleeping, that's when their brain is filing away all the things they learned while awake. When those memories are stored away, they can easily be recalled when a situation requires that information.

How Much Sleep Do You and Your Child Need?

Families often ask me if their child is getting enough sleep each night. These guidelines will give you an idea if you and your child are sleeping within the range of normal. As the typical sleep durations are quite broad, chances are your child is getting enough sleep. Are you?

1 TO 2 MONTHS: 10½ to 18 hours per 24 hours

3 TO 11 MONTHS: 9 to 12 hours at night; one to four 30-minute to 2-hour naps a day

12 TO 18 MONTHS: 9 to 12 hours at night; two naps up to 1½ hours each per day

18 MONTHS TO 3 YEARS: 9 to 12 hours at night; one nap up to 2 hours per day

3 TO 5 YEARS: 11 to 13 hours at night

5 TO 12 YEARS: 9 to 11 hours at night

12 TO 18 YEARS: 8 to 10 hours at night

18 YEARS AND OVER: 7 to 9 hours at night

Emotional Responses to Lack of Sleep

A lack of sleep also affects us emotionally. We're more likely to experience low moods, anxiety, stress, and symptoms of depression if we're not consistently getting enough sleep. We're less likely to want to socialize when those issues surface, which can increase feelings of isolation and loneliness, creating a hard-to-break cycle.

Your child may be cranky without enough sleep, not wanting to be apart from you and needing you to entertain them, which they can't do for themselves when they're overtired. They become bored quickly and need you to help them, which often means you can't set them down for even a minute.

The Signs of Tiredness

How do you know if your child needs more sleep than they are getting? Remember, we all want to be tired *before* we lie down for sleep, so don't look at how tired you or your child is right before sleep. Instead, look at the level of tiredness midway through the awake period. How tired does your child seem between naps? Look for the following signs of tiredness:

Acting "grumpy"

Becoming quiet

Looking "glassy-eyed"

Loud chatting or babbling

Pulling on ears

Rubbing eyes

Seeming distant or "spaced out"

Are they showing any of these signs at times when they should normally be wide-awake? If so, your child needs more sleep.

As for you and your level of tiredness, check in with yourself mid-morning and midafternoon. You can better gauge if you are getting enough sleep at these times than you can first thing in the morning, when you are naturally going to be tired; after lunch, when we all come to a natural lull; or just before bed, which is when you want to be tired.

How Baby Sleep Changes Over Time

Newborns are generally great sleepers and can sleep for hours and hours and hours—being born is exhausting work! It doesn't remain this way for very long: As a child grows, they can stay awake for longer periods. A newborn may barely be able to stay awake for a feed, but over the coming months, sleep will develop and change dramatically, and awake periods will gradually get longer and longer. Within the first nine months, your child's sleep will shift from sleeping nearly all the time to taking just two naps a day and hopefully getting nice long stretches at night. It's worth remembering that each of us has an optimal amount of sleep we need to function at our best, and children, even babies, are the same.

Newborn

Newborns are great at napping, and in fact, that's all they do. They nap for an hour or two around the clock, both day and night. Hungry tummies prevent them from sleeping longer, and that's okay. Just think about how small their tummy is. At birth, it's the size of an olive, and it's going to need to be filled up often. At two weeks, your child's stomach will have more than doubled its capacity and is about the size of an egg. That's still pretty small and will still need to be refilled often. You may need to refill that little tummy every two or three hours. It's normal for your child to wake for this. Avoid thinking that giving them a bigger feed will mean that they sleep longer; in fact, overfeeding can cause the opposite to happen. They're going to be uncomfortable with an overfilled belly, which can prevent them from sleeping.

You can expect your newborn to sleep about 16 hours per 24 hours; this is split pretty evenly between day and night. Night sleep begins to develop around six weeks, and when it does you may gradually see some longer stretches at night.

There is a significant shift with your child's sleep around 12 weeks; this is measured from your child's due date, not birth date. So, if your child was born two weeks earlier than their due date, this shift would develop a little later; you'd notice changes around 14 weeks. If your child was born late, you might see changes in sleep a little earlier. Around this time, they will stop having newborn sleep cycles; they now go through the same sleep cycles you and I go through—adult sleep cycles (which are 90 minutes), only shorter. That means they are now getting into a deep sleep and have the same REM (Rapid Eye Movement) dream sleep just like we do, though what babies are dreaming of we will never know.

After 12 weeks, your child produces a higher level of melatonin, the hormone that induces sleep, when they are placed in a dark or dim area. The higher level will help your child fall asleep and remain asleep. As night sleep continues to develop, we start to see sleep cycles consolidating. We may see the opposite happen with naps, and they're becoming more of a challenge. Those naps may now be a maximum of just one sleep cycle, which is usually between 30 and 45 minutes.

AT THREE MONTHS OLD, your child will need about 15 hours of sleep per 24 hours: 9 or 10 hours at night and between 4 and 5 hours of daily naps.

4 to 6 Months

Awake times will continue to lengthen, and naps will feel more consistent. Finally, your day will begin to feel a little more predictable. You may still be struggling with those short naps, but sometime between the ages of four and six months, they will begin to develop, and when they develop, your child can consolidate sleep cycles; this may mean longer naps.

Naps develop individually; the first nap of the day is likely the first to get easier. Your child will not take a long time to fall asleep following your nap routine, and they will begin to nap for up to an hour and a half. Shortly after the first nap has developed and lengthened, you'll notice the same with the second and then the third.

AT FOUR TO SIX MONTHS OLD, your child will need about 14 hours of sleep per 24 hours: 10 hours at night and 4 hours of daily naps, usually spread out between three and four naps.

6 to 12 Months

During this period, night sleep cycles continue to consolidate; most children are sleeping through the night, though we need to take into consideration what sleeping through the night actually means. Sleeping through the night, according to sleep researchers, is six or more consecutive hours of sleep without parents' help. Personally, that's not what I call sleeping through the night. A child who falls asleep at 7:00 p.m. and wakes for a feed six and a half hours later, at 1:30 a.m., has not slept through the night. What I consider sleeping through the night is when the child sleeps through the *entire* night without needing help.

Waking during the night is quite normal within this age range, and so is needing to feed during the night. Often, well-meaning family and friends tell new parents that their child doesn't need to feed during the night because they have reached some magical age or weight. That's just not true; there is no set weight, age, or medical or scientific rule for when a baby no longer needs to feed during the night. Some babies can go the entire night without a feed at 12 weeks, and some are nearer to nine months when this occurs. If your child continues to feed through the night, it doesn't mean anything is wrong. Their temperament will play a large part in this, as will how much milk or formula they consume each day, how much one-on-one time they have with parents, how they napped during the day, and so much more.

There are a few things to remember about this age range: When a child has the ability to get themselves to sleep, they will also have the ability to get themselves back to sleep if they don't need help (that

REAL-LIFE STORY

When Sarah and David brought baby Jessica home from the hospital, they were determined to get Jessica onto a daily routine and set up positive sleep habits right away. Of course, Jessica had other ideas; she struggled to stay awake after a feed, would spend much longer feeding than Sarah and David had anticipated, and did not want to be put down in her bassinet at all. Sarah and David were getting frustrated and thought they must be doing something wrong.

I advised the new parents to take a little step back and follow Jessica's lead. Jessica knew when she was hungry, and because she was trying to establish Sarah's milk supply, she would spend a long time feeding. When they were not struggling to follow a plan, their baby had a much easier time relaxing and sleeping, and could easily be lain in her bassinet for sleep. Sarah and David no longer felt like they were fighting a losing battle; they were working as a team with Jessica.

When Jessica reached 12 weeks, we began working on a routine, and Jessica had a much easier time adjusting to the daily schedule Sarah and David were implementing.

is, when they don't need a diaper change or a feed). Most children who have the skills to get themselves to sleep will have minimal feeds throughout the night as a result.

AT SIX TO TWELVE MONTHS, your child will continue to need about 14 hours of sleep per 24 hours. The majority of this sleep is at night, with around 3 hours of total nap sleep. A six-month-old will nap three times a day, dropping down to two naps around seven months.

12 Months and Beyond

Your child will drop down to one nap sometime around 15 months; they will usually take this nap after lunch. They'll continue to need about 11 hours of sleep at night, and as they grow, gradually reduce the amount they are napping. Naps are dropped completely sometime between three and six years old.

I believe we can eliminate night feeds for all children when they reach the one-year-old mark. Now, solid foods are not supplementing milk or formula feeds; they are having more and more solid foods and consume a whole range of different foods. A child will still need to have breast milk or formula throughout the day, but not so much at night.

Naps versus Night Sleeps

Night sleeps start developing at six weeks, but naps don't begin to develop until sometime between four and six months; this can cause naps and night sleep to look wildly different. Your child may have a much easier time napping during the day and struggle to get longer stretches of sleep at night. Or it can be the opposite: They have a much harder time with their naps, and sleep much easier at night, getting long stretches of sleep. Try not to worry, as both of these scenarios are normal. Struggling with one area of sleep is not something that lasts forever. Naps and night sleep develop at different ages as well as at different paces, which I'll discuss more later.

The Importance of Naps

Naps may feel like a luxury to us adults, but they are vitally important for your child. Young children are not biologically able to stay awake for long periods; they *must* nap. The naps give your child's brain and body the opportunity to rest and recharge.

If your child has ever skipped a nap, you know firsthand how challenging the day can get. Your child will be less patient, whether with feeds, playing with you, or entertaining themselves. They will need to be entertained more, and this constant entertainment can lead to overstimulation as well as to overtiredness. Being overstimulated and overtired is going to make the next nap or falling asleep at the beginning of the night more challenging. Your child will struggle to unwind. It may seem like they suddenly have a second wind; you know they're tired, but they appear to be full of energy. Then suddenly they'll crash hard, often in floods of tears. Even now, they may struggle to fall asleep—all because they missed a nap.

It's not just their mood that is impacted when they miss a nap; your child will have a harder time remembering things. As you've learned, when your child is well rested, they have an easier time recalling what they have been learning.

The Challenges of Sleep Regression

How is it that a regression comes along just when you think your child's sleep is beginning to settle down? Regressions happen periodically throughout the first two years. There's a good reason for them and, thankfully, they don't last forever.

A regression occurs when your child is working on new skills. This could be a physical skill that is easy for you to see, such as rolling, sitting up, crawling, or walking. It may be language development, where your child is making many more sounds, having an explosion in the number of words they are using, or beginning to string sentences together. When it comes to brain development, it is much harder to determine what is happening. They are learning problem-solving—for example, when they hit the wooden brick on the high chair tray, it makes a noise, but not when they hit in on the carpet. You may not physically see what your child is learning, but they are still learning.

Children have periods when they knuckle down and work on one skill. When they are learning to roll, it's as if they can think of nothing else. Whenever you lay them down, they just have to roll. That can certainly make for some interesting diaper changes, I can tell you! You lay them down and they try and try to roll onto their tummy. They may get stuck on their side, leading to a lot of frustration. You roll them onto their back again and they proceed to roll onto their side again, leading to frustration for all. Children have an innate desire to practice these new skills, and it's pretty impressive that they do. Just think about all that a child learns, practices, and perfects in the first year or two. It's impressive! If we continued this behavior into adulthood, think about how many things we would be amazing at because we kept working on something until we perfected it.

Because a child is learning a new skill and can't *not* practice it whenever they have the opportunity to do so, sleep is going to get a little wonky. Your child wants to practice these new skills everywhere: the floor, during a diaper change, in the bath, as well as in the bed, which can be at the expense of sleep.

Luckily, children mostly develop at around the same rate and work on these new skills at similar ages so we can predict, more or less, when a regression is going to hit. The first sleep regression happens at around four months and is a continuation of the big shift that occurred with sleep at about 12 weeks. Your little one can have a harder time falling asleep at the start of the night; they may have long awake periods in which a quick feed that once helped them back to sleep no longer works. And naps? They may reduce in duration; those two-hour naps are long gone, and your child may now only manage 45 minutes.

The next regression hits somewhere around the eight- or nine-month mark. This regression can last up to six weeks. A lot is happening developmentally at this age. Your child is about to enter a significant stage of separation anxiety that begins when your child starts moving. Learning these new skills—as when learning any new skill—can also be a reason for a sleep regression. Your child may be pulling up on furniture, or even learning to walk or crawl. Physical development, cognitive development, and separation anxiety make for quite the regression.

Just when you were feeling that you'd settled into a routine following the nine-month regression, the twelve-month regression begins. Thankfully, this regression is nowhere near as challenging as the last one. This regression usually impacts naps, where your child has a tougher time sleeping throughout the day. If they are not napping great, they are going to have a harder time at night because, as you now understand, an overtired child will struggle to fall asleep and remain asleep.

The next regression is at around 18 months; this is when things become interesting. An eighteen-month-old is a very opinionated human being, especially when it comes to getting into bed and falling asleep. They know what they want and what they don't want, and aren't afraid to share their opinions with you. I'm sorry to be the bearer of bad news, but one more regression occurs at around two years old. This regression is much like the eighteen-month regression. Your two-year-old is quite sure you are not the boss of them and that sleep is for wimps! You'll learn more about sleep regression in chapter 5.

EXERCISE:
Mindful Breathing to Relieve Stress

There is no doubt about it: Parenting is stressful, and you may feel that things are out of your control. This simple breathing exercise can help you feel more grounded and help relax you in a stressful situation. Don't worry; this will only take a few minutes, and you can do this almost anywhere.

1. Sit or stand comfortably. Close your eyes if you like.

2. Take a deep breath in slowly through your nose and let it out through your mouth. Continue to breathe at this pace, being mindful of your breath.

3. As you breathe in, pay attention to your chest and stomach expanding. As you breathe out, notice how your chest and stomach contract. Feel your chest and stomach rising as you breathe in and lowering as you breathe out.

4. If thoughts come to you, push them away and return your focus to your breath. Continue this process for a few minutes.

Even a couple minutes of mindful breathing can help you feel calmer, more relaxed, and better able to handle a situation, including sleep difficulties.

Sleepy Baby, Happy Family

When your child is getting the best sleep possible, that means you are also getting the best sleep possible. That can translate into having a much easier time going about your daily routines and enjoying yourself and your family as much as you can during the process. Yes, there will be the normal challenges, but struggling with sleep will not be one of them. When you put in consistent effort, better sleep will be on the horizon for you. However, your child's sleep is as unique as they are; they will develop at their own pace. There's no guarantee they will sleep through the night at some specified time, but there is plenty you can do to help them reach this goal when it is developmentally appropriate for them to do so. You'll be learning easy-to-follow techniques and strategies throughout this book. Just stay with it.

Conclusion

Your child's sleep will develop and change so much over the first few years of their life. Starting with shorter periods of sleep where everything is a nap, to the development of bedtime and naptimes. Sleep is something that is always evolving and developing. In the next chapter, you'll learn the ins and outs of sleep training.

Chapter 2

Sleep Training 101

THE SLEEP-TRAINING TECHNIQUES DISCUSSED IN this chapter are methods you can use to teach your child the skills not only to get themselves to sleep at bedtime but also to get back to sleep throughout the night. There are no one-size-fits-all approaches to sleep training; every child is unique. As you read about these techniques, you'll most likely gravitate toward one or two in particular. You know what's likely to work for your child and your family. Later chapters break down the techniques and cover the best ways to prepare you and your child for sleep training. I know you're motivated and want to get started now, but taking the time to understand the different methods and developing a plan will bring you less stress and a much easier time sleep training.

What Is Sleep Training?

When we sleep train, we are teaching a child the skills they need to get themselves to sleep and, therefore, back to sleep when they naturally wake during the night. Humans can wake as many as six times a night, so waking is not the issue; it's needing help getting back to sleep that may be the problem. When a child has the skills to get to sleep, they can get themselves comfortably back to sleep when they naturally rouse throughout the night. It's worth noting again that there is no magical age, weight, or developmental stage when a child no longer needs to feed during the night. (There's more on this later.)

The Origins of Sleep Training

One of the earliest parenting books that mentions sleep training is *The Care and Feeding of Children* by American pediatrician Luther Emmett Holt in 1894, revised in 1907. In this book, Holt suggested putting your child into bed "comfortable . . . and awake." It is also recommended to *not* rock your child to sleep or help your child to sleep in any way, and if your child is comfortable, they should be left to "cry it out."

Over the past 100 years, our attitudes toward sleep training have changed slightly, and though Cry-It-Out is a technique that parents may continue to use, the way we support children as they learn these new skills has changed. We understand that helping our children learn something new can speed up the learning process. Being there and helping your child is probably something you want to do.

A century ago, parenting experts thought it was a good idea to leave children in their crib to cry; they believed it was good for their lungs. We know that's not the case; aside from their very first time, crying does not help your child's lungs at all.

The Key Principles

Each sleep-training technique has its own rules. Once you are familiar with them, you'll know which technique is going to be a better fit for your child. The best technique for your child is the one you can follow through on from start to finish, that you feel comfortable with, and that you can be consistent with night after night. No matter which technique you choose, keep the following in mind before you get started.

Commit to a Strategy

You will probably gravitate toward a sleep-training method you think is going to work for your child's unique temperament, which I'll help you identify in the upcoming exercise. Commit to this technique. Sleep training doesn't achieve immediate results, so you'll be working with the method for several nights before you begin to see any change.

Be Consistent

Now that you've committed to sleep training, you'll want to be consistent and follow through. Don't give up. It's not fair to make your child feel frustrated (as sleep training almost inevitably does) and then give in. Sleep training will take much longer if you are inconsistent because your child won't know what to expect. Only start sleep training if you are prepared to be consistent.

Get on the Same Page

One parent shouldn't assume the other parent knows what's going on when it comes to sleep training. Iron things out *before* you get started. Discuss your goals, the technique you've chosen, what you each need to do, and when you need to do it. You'll reach your goals quicker if you operate as a team.

Stay Calm

Try to remain as calm and relaxed as possible throughout the process. It's not easy, I know. Your child can pick up on your emotions; if you are stressed and tense, they will be as well. Talk quietly and reassuringly to your child, and don't try to talk over them. This will help you both remain as calm as possible. I've included a few calming exercises you can try if you feel you need a time-out. You can find them on pages 4, 17, 38, 64, 105, and 117.

EXERCISE:
Identify Your Child's Temperament

Your child's unique temperament will play a part in how they sleep as well as how they will best learn to sleep more independently. Identifying your child's unique temperament will help you determine which sleep training technique works best for your family. The three main temperaments are: 1) laid-back and easygoing; 2) slow to warm up or shy; and 3) spirited and more intense. The following table will help you figure out which temperamental type your child matches.

	LAID-BACK AND EASYGOING	SLOW TO WARM UP OR SHY	SPIRITED AND MORE INTENSE
Rhythm for feeding and sleeping	Set your watch; predictable	Ordinarily predictable	Unpredictable
Openness to new people	Will go to anyone	Seems terrified; takes a long time to warm up	Quickly warms up
Adaptability to new situations	Changes on a dime	Unsettled for a while	Can take a little while to feel settled

	LAID-BACK AND EASYGOING	SLOW TO WARM UP OR SHY	SPIRITED AND MORE INTENSE
Emotional drama	Calm most of the time	Ordinary highs and lows	Emotional roller coaster
Attention span and focus	Focused, but can be easily distracted	Focused, but can be easily distracted	Locked in and reluctant to switch
Level of pickiness and rigidity	Most things are fine	Know what they like but can be easily distracted	Know what they like and what they don't like; not afraid to share feelings
Sleep notes	Have a much easier time establishing routines; adapt quickly and easily when you introduce a daily routine, as well as nap and bed-time routines. Have a slightly easier time learning new sleep skills.	Struggle a little more with changes that introduce something new, such as sleep training. May seem unsettled and will let you know when they are feeling this way.	Very alert and reactions to things are intense (from very sad to hyster-ically funny); have a tougher time switching off and slowing down, which can make sleep more of a struggle; thrive on the predict-ability of routines (knowing what will happen next is more relaxing).

Your child will likely fall into more than one category. They may be more laid-back and easygoing when it comes to meeting new people and going to new places, but more spirited and intense when it comes to sleep. Don't worry if they seem to be a mix; you want to work with your child and their unique temperament with everything you do, not just sleep. If your child is shy when it comes to meeting new people, stay close when you visit family. If they are spirited when it comes to sleep, you'll want to help them relax before you begin your nap and bedtime routines.

The Benefits

I'm sure you can guess a few benefits of sleep training: Both you and your child will feel well rested. Being tired and sleep deprived is hard on us. Life is certainly more manageable when we don't need to get up repeatedly every single night for months on end to attend to a child who can't get back to sleep.

A child who sleeps more independently has a much easier time when they encounter regular sleep disturbances, such as after a stimulating day, attending a new daycare, or travel, as well as when they are going through a sleep regression. Let's say your child is waking five times a night and they have a sleep regression. Naturally, they will wake up more often during the regression, maybe eight or more times a night. Or if your child is sleeping through the night or waking once, they may wake once or twice a night when going through a sleep regression. If they are teething or unwell, there's a similar effect. The benefit during these times is that they have been learning the skills to get themselves to sleep and back to sleep, so they will have a much easier time doing so even when they are slightly uncomfortable.

The Pitfalls

Sleep training is not a quick fix; it may take hours over many nights. There isn't anything you can do that will make your child sleep through the night or fall asleep within seconds of getting into bed. The pitfall here is that you might erroneously think what you're doing isn't working because it requires a lot of consistent, committed effort.

Beth was desperate; her four-month-old was waking almost hourly from 8:00 p.m. to 6:00 a.m. She knew she needed to do something about it. Beth found a sleep-training technique she was comfortable implementing and knew would work for her child. After spending a couple of weeks tweaking her daily routine, nap routine, and bedtime routine, she began sleep training. Beth started to see results on night three. Her four-month-old started sleeping for longer stretches. Within a week, Beth's daughter was getting herself to sleep with minimal help, waking twice during the night for a quick feed, and was able to get herself back to sleep. As Beth's daughter grew, she knew her child was feeding enough during the day, and she was able to gradually reduce night feeds.

Give it at least a week. If you are not seeing any improvement at all, stop the technique. Don't start using a different technique right away because this can be confusing to your child. Wait a week or two before trying again with a different technique.

Thinking that once your child has a consistent sleep routine, you'll never need to sleep train again is another pitfall. Sleep doesn't remain static; it's always developing. As your child grows, their sleep needs will change, and they will inevitably go through sleep regressions (see chapter 5 for more on this). With all these regressions, you may wonder if sleep training is worth it since sleep will become unsettled again. Don't let regressions put you off. The better your child is sleeping, the less of a negative impact a regression will have.

The Myths

Here are a few sleep-training myths that I hear regularly, along with my myth-busting responses:

MYTH: *Sleep training will involve letting your child "cry it out."*

This is a big fear of many parents who approach sleep training. There are many different techniques; you don't need to walk out on a crying child and ignore their cries when teaching them the skills to get themselves to sleep.

MYTH: *Sleep training will eliminate all night feeds.*

Some children will need to continue to feed through the night. When a child has the skills to get themselves to sleep when they are not hungry, they will have the skills to get themselves back to sleep without relying on a feed.

MYTH: *They will eventually grow out of needing to be helped to sleep.*

Yes, they may learn the skills on their own, but if we do not give them help early on, there is no way to know when that will be. It could be in a week, a month, a year, or several years. In some cases, five- and six-year-olds still need to learn the skills to get themselves to sleep and back to sleep when they wake.

MYTH: *If I don't start sleep training by a certain age, it will be too late.*

This is not true, though some ages are easier when it comes to learning independent sleep skills; your child is never too old, and you haven't missed the window.

Different Approaches to Sleep Training

There are several methods promoted by different experts. One writer or another may attach a cute name to this technique or that one, but there really are just a few basic strategies, which I'll cover here. One of these will be right for you and your child. Let's take a look.

Cry-It-Out Method

"Cry-It-Out" was popularized by Richard Ferber, MD, in his 1985 book *Solve Your Child's Sleep Problems*. It is often called the Ferber method or even Ferberization. In this method, crying is expected, but it's time limited. Crying time is gradually increased until the child settles.

This technique works best for children who are more laid-back and easygoing, and over six months of age. This technique doesn't work well for children who are more intense and spirited; they don't soothe easily when the cry has become urgent.

This method requires attention to the clock. You may find a timer helpful. Here's a typical schedule for the Cry-It-Out method:

NIGHT 1: Following your bedtime routine, place your child in their crib while they are still awake. Leave the room.

If your child begins to cry, stay out of your child's room for 5 minutes. After 5 minutes, go into the room and soothe your child for 1–2 minutes. Don't pick them up to soothe, but you can place your hands on them. After a minute or two, leave the room again.

This time, wait 10 minutes before you go back into your child's room to soothe them. Hands-on soothing is okay, but picking up to soothe is not. Again, remain for a minute or two and then leave the room.

Now, wait 15 minutes before returning to soothe for a minute or two. The maximum time you will be out of the room is 15 minutes.

If you think your child is falling asleep (that is, they've quieted down), allow 10 minutes for them to fall asleep before going in to check on them. Some parents simply look at the video monitor and don't enter the room again until necessary. You can continue to enter your child's room to soothe them if you need to at the established intervals.

NIGHT 2: Following your bedtime routine, place your child in their crib while they are still awake. Leave the room. If your child begins to cry, stay out of your child's room for 10 minutes before returning to soothe for 1–2 minutes. (Remember, no picking up, rocking, or feeding.) Increase to 15 minutes and repeat this process until your child has fallen asleep.

NIGHT 3: Following your bedtime routine, place your child in their crib while they are still awake. Leave the room. If your child begins to cry, stay out of your child's room for 15 minutes before soothing for 1–2 minutes.

(Remember, no picking up, rocking, or feeding.) Repeat this process until your child has fallen asleep.

If you are still having night feeds, use the same technique when your child wakes throughout the night and it is not a feed time. There's more on night feeds in chapter 3.

Tippy-Toe-Out Method

With this technique, you maintain a close presence but avoid picking up your child until their crying becomes urgent. This method works nicely for all temperaments of children. We can get started with laid-back children from four months and more intense and slower-to-warm-up children from six months. Here's how this technique works:

Start by positioning a comfortable chair next to the crib. Test out this chair beforehand to make sure you can comfortably sit in it for a while without straining your back, even with your hands through the bars or over the rail.

NIGHTS 1, 2, AND 3: Lay your child in the crib close enough that you can reach them from your chair. Touch your child gently and use your voice to soothe; you can talk, shush, or sing. You can pat your child, but try not to pat in a rhythm because when you stop, it will be more noticeable.

If your child stands up, lay them straight back down. If your child is really upset, indicated by an urgent cry, you can pick them up, remaining next to the crib. When they have soothed, lay them back down in the crib and sit in your chair, placing your hands on your child as needed. Repeat as many times as required.

Remain in the chair until your child is fully asleep, but don't rush off as soon as you see them close their eyes, as they are likely to wake instantly. Ten minutes seems to be the magic number when it comes to moving after your child has fallen asleep.

NIGHTS 4, 5, AND 6: Move the chair a small distance away from the crib. Lay your child in the crib and sit in the chair; you can talk, sing, or shush to soothe your child. Try to remain in the chair as much as possible. If your child cries a little, try to stay in the chair and soothe with your voice. If the cry becomes more urgent, you can go to your child to help soothe them, even picking them up if needed. Always place them back down into the crib and go back to the chair when they are comforted. Tiptoe out of the room when they are settled and seem ready to fall asleep.

NIGHTS 7, 8, AND 9: Move the chair farther away, right by the door if you can (but don't block your exit!). Lay your child down as before and use your voice as needed to soothe and reassure. Intervene as little as possible and stay in the chair as much as you can. As soon as your child seems settled and ready to fall asleep, tiptoe out of the room.

If you are still having night feeds, use the same technique when your child wakes throughout the night and it is not a feed time. There's more on night feeds in chapter 3.

Pat-the-Baby Method

This gentle method ensures your baby is asleep before you leave the room. It's especially helpful for babies four to six months old and works for all temperaments. The key to making this method work is your ability to remain calm, quiet, and very patient.

To begin, lay your child in their crib on their side. Make sure they can't roll onto their stomach by placing your hand on their chest. Lean over the crib (this can be a little backbreaking, sorry) and firmly pat your child's back, patting (nonrhythmically as much as possible) between the shoulder blades. You need to shush (a long drawn out *shhhhhhhhh*) past your child's ear, not directly into it. This isn't always the easiest thing to do; don't injure yourself and don't shush too loudly into your child's ears.

If your child doesn't settle, pick them up and hold them to your shoulder. You can continue to pat and shush. When your baby has relaxed and their breathing evens out, lay them back in the crib, continuing to pat and shush.

If your child stays quiet, start to slow the patting to a stop, but continue to shush for about 5 more minutes. If your child remains calm, slow the patting and stop the shushing. It can take up to 20 minutes for your child to fall asleep, so don't rush off. Your child is in a deeper sleep when their body relaxes and their breathing slows.

Important: *Make sure you gently roll your child onto their back before you leave.*

When your baby is older than six months, you can change this technique slightly as follows:

Lay your child in the crib. There is a good chance your child will cry, roll over, sit up, or even stand when you try to leave, but try anyway.

If your child cries, begin by soothing your child with your voice, but if they continue to cry, pick them up. Hold them in a horizontal position and don't let them fall asleep on you.

When they stop crying, immediately lay them back down. Lay them on their side and place your hand on their chest, so they don't roll onto their stomach. Reassure them that it is okay by talking to them calmly. Rub your child's back, pat gently between the shoulder blades, or maintain a gentle pressure.

When your child seems to have settled, gradually withdraw your hand and back slowly away. You can talk soothingly to let your child know you are still there.

Your child may realize you have moved away and may begin to fuss. If your child rolls around, sits up, or stands, wait until you need to help before going back to the crib and restarting the process. I know it can be tempting to rush and help your child as soon as they begin to move. Children may sometimes check what's going on and then settle themselves, so don't be too quick to intervene.

If you are making the move to lay your child down and they begin to cry, continue the process of laying them down. Then, after they are down, you can pick them up right away if you need to.

If you are still having night feeds, use the same technique when your child wakes throughout the night and it is not a feed time. There's more on night feeds in chapter 3.

The Michi Method

This method, which I developed, works for laid-back children from four months up and more intense/spirited and slow-to-warm-up children from six months. The Michi method lets you soothe however you and your child prefer. You will remove one of your soothing supports every fourth night until your child is settling on their own. This method has four keys:

1. Respond immediately to your child's urgent cry. Do not respond to fussing or whining.

2. Be hands-off until it is clear your child is getting sleepy.

3. Stay attuned to your child's preferences for soothing.

4. Remove one way you are helping your child every fourth night.

Go through your regular bedtime routine and lay your child in their crib, not nursing, rocking, or bouncing your child to sleep.

Begin by soothing your child with your voice. If the cry becomes more urgent, pick your child up. Soothe your child however you can—bounce, rock, sing, or talk. Continue until your child has calmed down or the cry has changed from urgent to fussy or whiny. Then lay them back in their crib.

Don't worry if they jump up, roll over, or get to sitting again. Simply lay them back down. At this stage, they are wondering why you are not helping them get to sleep like you always have. If your child is sitting or standing in the crib and doesn't need picking up to soothe, lay them back down every three to five minutes.

It's fine to talk to your child to settle them, and you may find being a little hands-on is helpful when it comes to soothing, so if it helps, you can gently touch your child at this point. If (or when) your child's cry becomes more urgent, pick them up and soothe until they are calm.

Don't mistake the mad or fussy cry for the urgent cry. An urgent cry, which reaches a fever pitch, doesn't stop the second you pick your child up, but an angry or fussy cry will. You will instinctively come to tell the difference without having to pick up your child to test it out.

Repeat, repeat, repeat until your child becomes sleepy. You can tell when your child grows tired because they won't jump up as quickly. They may roll around, rub their head against the mattress, or seem to slow down physically; this is your cue for a change in tactic. Now you want to lean over the bed and be hands-on. You can rub their head or chest, or pat their back. Singing, talking, or shushing may also help your child sleep.

Don't rush off as soon as your child has fallen asleep. Continue to pat until they are in a deeper sleep, up to 10 minutes, and then gradually stop your help: First discontinue the talking, singing, or shushing; after a few minutes, stop the patting or rubbing, but keep your hands on your child for a minute or two and then lift your hands.

Every fourth night, eliminate an aspect of how you were helping your child get to sleep. You can start by removing either the patting or the shushing. After four nights of the reduced pattern, eliminate one more element. Continue removing elements every fourth night until your child is getting to sleep without any help from you.

If you are still having night feeds, use the same technique when your child wakes throughout the night and it is not a feed time. There's more on night feeds in chapter 3.

When Is a Good Time to Start?

When to start sleep training depends on the technique you will be using as well as your child's temperament. In general:

○ You can begin sleep training using a gentle technique with a child who is more laid-back and easygoing after four months. Try Pat-the-Baby, Tippy-Toe-Out, or the Michi method.

○ Wait until six months before using Cry-It-Out.

○ Children who are more intense and spirited should wait until six months before starting with a gentle technique; avoid Cry-It-Out altogether.

○ Although there is no perfect age to begin sleep training, it's going to feel a little easier when your child is under 12 months. But that doesn't mean you can't use these techniques with older children. The only difference is that older children may protest more.

EXERCISE: Visualize Your Ideal Outcome

If sleep training feels overwhelming and you're not sure you have the energy to move forward, take a few minutes to think about how you will feel when your child can get themselves to sleep at the beginning of the night. Here's how:

1. Find a quiet place to sit, close your eyes, and focus on your breath.

2. In your mind's eye, visualize how your evening will go while your child is asleep. See yourself enjoying your evening and doing whatever it is that brings you satisfaction.

3. See yourself waking up in the morning after your child has been sleeping for longer stretches at night and, as a result, your family is getting a better night's sleep. How do you feel? How will your day be different? See yourself moving through your day with more ease.

4. When you're ready, take a deep breath, remind yourself of the goal and know that your sleep-training efforts will be worth it, and then open your eyes.

Feeding to Sleep?

If you have been feeding your child to sleep, you need to get a few things in place before you start sleep training. You can't simply avoid the feed at the end of the day as your child will likely wake hungry, but you do want to avoid feeding your child to sleep or drowsiness.

Feed your child just before you begin your bedtime routine. You may want to go somewhere quiet and calm, so they are not distracted and they take a good feed. Then, go through all the steps of your bedtime routine, and then offer another feed. As your child has already had a good feed, this is just a "top-off." Your child shouldn't fall asleep while feeding and shouldn't get too drowsy.

Before you begin sleep training, you can help your child get to sleep while holding or gently rocking them. I've found that the feeding-to-sleep habit is one of the hardest to break; don't worry, you aren't replacing one sleep crutch with another. Holding or slowly rocking your child to sleep is an easier habit for your child to break when you begin sleep training.

It's Okay to Feel Anxious and Overwhelmed

Starting anything new can cause anxiety, and sleep training is no exception. When you first get started, you don't know how your child is going to react. You're not even sure how *you* are going to react. Will you be able to keep your cool? Here's the thing: You won't know until you get started. So have a plan in place and make sure you are confident that what you (and your partner) need to be doing and when is clear to each of you. If you have a solid plan to stick to, you won't feel as anxious and overwhelmed as you would if you went into sleep training blindly.

Build Your Self-Esteem as a Parent

You may be reading a lot of information in books and online about child development, sleep, diapers, illnesses—anything and everything related to your child. You're probably coming across a lot of contradictory advice, which makes what to do very confusing. One important way to avoid confusion and reduce overwhelming feelings is to trust your gut instinct. The more you trust your gut, the more you will trust yourself to do the best thing for your child, and the more your self-esteem as a parent will grow.

You are the expert in your child; you know them better than anyone else does, so you have a pretty good idea if something will work with them. Parental instinct has helped the human race for thousands of years, long before we had parenting books and the internet! If something feels right to you in your gut, it's the right thing for your child. If something makes you feel uncomfortable and icky inside, chances are it's not right for you or your child. Don't make knee-jerk decisions; let something sit with you and then decide if you think it will work for your family.

Remember: You Are in Control

You get to determine your child's daily schedule and set their bedtime. You get to choose the best method for helping them get to sleep and back to sleep when they wake up throughout the night. You get to decide what outfit your child will wear—unless, of course, you have a fashion-opinionated toddler. Even then, you're still the one who chooses which clothing they have to pick from. These are your choices, and there will be many more choices to make as your child grows. You are in control of how you parent your child.

Although you may not feel like you are in control—and, it's true, you are not in control of *everything*—you are in control of much more than you think. Aside from being in control of making the choices I've already mentioned, you are in control of one more very important thing: how you react. I understand that it's not always easy to remain calm, but you can make the choice to take a time-out if you need one. There are several exercises included in this book for regaining your calm. See pages 4, 17, 38, 64, 105, and 117.

How to Approach Your Plan

Helping your child have a better night's sleep doesn't mean you are only working with your child at the beginning of the night. To make sleep training as easy as possible for your family, look at sleep as a whole, naps *and* bedtime and the situations surrounding them. Regardless of the sleep-training technique you will be using, there are other elements you will want to work on that will help you reach your goals sooner.

For starters, you want to create an ideal sleep environment that feels safe to your child. You need to help your child relax so that they have an easier time falling asleep. You want to feel comfortable reducing the night feeds and then eliminating them altogether. This is all broken down into bite-size pieces over the next few chapters so you can easily get started sleep training, as follows:

○ In chapter 3, you'll learn how to create the perfect sleep environment, an ideal daily routine, and a relaxing bedtime routine to help your child fall asleep with ease.

○ In chapter 4, you'll learn how to implement your chosen sleep-training technique with as much ease as possible.

○ In chapter 5, you'll receive the encouragement you need to remain consistent now that your child is getting better sleep. Having a plan in place will mean your child has fewer hiccups when life gets in the way and tries to mess with their sleep.

Set Realistic Expectations

As you've learned, there are no quick fixes or one-size-fits-all approaches when it comes to your child's sleep. Their sleep may become even more challenging before you see some improvement; this is normal. You are not helping your child get back to sleep as quickly as possible; instead, you're breaking habits and teaching new skills, which takes time and effort. You can expect the first few nights to be challenging. You should begin to see some improvements regardless of which technique you use (as long as the technique works for your child's temperament) within three to four nights. But give it at least a week. Any small improvement is a step in the right direction.

Celebrate Small Successes Along the Way

Don't wait until your child is successfully sleeping through the night to celebrate your accomplishments. There are many steps on the road to sleeping through the night, and each step is a step in the right direction and should be celebrated. If your child was waking every hour, but now they are sleeping for three-hour stretches, celebrate! No, that's not sleeping through the night, but it is two hours more than they were sleeping before you got started. Remember, the goal is progress, not perfection.

Conclusion

You may be leaning more toward one of the sleep-training techniques in this chapter—that's great. Don't worry if you're not. As you read the following chapters, you may decide on a technique. If you're still undecided, you can always reread the technique descriptions in this chapter and then make your decision.

Chapter 3

Set Yourself (and Your Baby) Up for Success

PREPARING YOUR CHILD FOR SLEEP TRAINING will help them have a much easier time breaking habits and learning new skills. Begin planning at least a week prior to starting sleep training. Think of this stage as building a solid foundation. Once this foundation has been established, you can continue to develop and move forward with sleep training. Don't skip this chapter; there's a lot to learn here that can make sleep training so much easier for your family.

Start When You Are Ready

There is no perfect time to begin sleep training; you'll know when you are ready. However, you'll want to avoid getting started under certain circumstances—for example, if your child is sick or in pain due to teething, it's worth waiting until they feel more comfortable. If your child is uncomfortable and in pain, they will have a harder time sleeping, which can make sleep training quite frustrating.

You also don't want to start too early (generally not before four months old). Make sure your child is feeding well and that you have created an emotional bond between you and your baby. This secure attachment, which usually happens around four months, is developed by:

○ Eye contact

○ Holding and cuddling your child

○ Responding to cries

○ Skin-to-skin contact

○ Speaking to your child with a calm, soothing voice

Your child's temperament will also play a part in when to get started. The more laid-back and easygoing your child is, the sooner you can begin. Laid-back children can start sleep training any time after four months. Children whose temperaments are more intense or slow to warm up will have a much easier time if you get started after six months.

Get Your Co-Parent or Support Team on Board

There's no reason to sleep train by yourself. This is a family project. If your child's other parent lives with you, enlist their help. You can take shifts at the beginning of the night (15 to 20 minutes is an excellent target) and then take turns when your child wakes during the night. When you are on your shift, you will be going into your child's room to soothe them. The help you provide will depend on the sleep-training technique you are using.

If you're on your own, get a friend or family member to help out—make an evening of it. Sleep training is so much easier if you have someone who can take a few turns and who can share in just how hard this can be in the beginning.

What If They Don't Agree?

Don't assume your co-parent knows what's going on or doesn't have an opinion on sleep training. Iron things out before you get started. Discuss the goals and the technique that will help you reach those goals. You may each need to compromise a little when it comes to choosing the sleep-training technique and developing your plan. You'll reach your goals quicker if you work together. There are several approaches to help your child sleep a little more independently, so try to find a method that works for both of you.

Sleep Training Alone

If you are sleep training solo, here are some tips that can make it a little easier for you:

○ Be well prepared before you begin sleep training. Don't start on a whim; you want to know what to do and exactly when to do it. Read through your sleep-training technique, and then reread it and let it sit with you for a day or two before starting.

○ Start sleep training on a night when you can rest the following day. If you have somewhere you need to be the next morning or an active day ahead, wait to get started on sleep training.

○ While you are sleep training, if you need to give yourself a time-out, take it. Sitting for even a few minutes in a quiet spot can help you feel a little more relaxed and better able to continue the technique.

○ Enroll an accountability partner; tell a friend or family member that you are planning to get started sleep training. Go over your plan and the process with them, and check in with them each morning. You are more likely to follow through if you have someone to report to.

Set Your Goals: What Does Success Look Like to You?

Think about where you are right now. Does your child need help falling asleep at the beginning of the night? Can your child only fall back asleep with you feeding or rocking them? Will your child only nap on you? Chances are you answered "yes" to one or more of these questions. After all, that's why you're reading this book!

When setting your goals, start by thinking about what "okay" sleep would look like for your child. It's not about your child sleeping perfectly; rather, it is something you could manage night in and night out. Maybe they need a little help getting to sleep at the beginning of the night. You could handle that. Or maybe your child wakes to feed before you go to bed and wakes once more during the night, falling back asleep quickly and easily after the feeds. You can handle that, too. Now, if you could wave a magic wand and alter your child's sleep, what would the best-case scenario look like? Would your child comfortably nap two or three times a day? Would they fall asleep within 10 minutes at night and sleep the entire night? How does your perfect night look?

Set goals somewhere between "okay" sleep and the "perfect" night. Of course, I would love for your best-case scenario to happen right away, but that may not be realistic for your child right now. It doesn't mean they won't reach those goals. For example, your child may still require a feed during the night. Remember, there is no magical age or developmental stage when a child no longer needs to feed during the night. If your child can get themselves to sleep at the beginning of the night and sleep well, waking once or twice for a needed feed, you're in good shape. If you set a goal for the best-case scenario, though, you'll miss out on all you've accomplished along the way. So find the sweet spot somewhere in the middle of "okay" and "perfect." You can always create new goals when smaller goals have been reached.

Your Sleep Goals

How do you set up a sleep goal for yourself when your child is not sleeping through the night? Remember, adults usually need between seven and eight hours of sleep at night. How much sleep are you getting? With a new baby, it will probably be a while before you are able to get a full night's sleep. However, you should still try to get the best possible sleep. This might mean that you need to go to bed early once or twice a week, or you might need to nap when the baby naps a few times a week. Maybe you can take turns with your partner sleeping in on the weekends. Set realistic sleep goals for yourself and try your best to achieve them. If you need help, ask.

EXERCISE: What Are Your Expectations for Yourself as a Parent?

I've mentioned various ways your child might behave when you are working on sleep training, but let's not forget about you. Understanding your emotions and how sleep training might make you feel will help you set realistic expectations for yourself during the process.

Answer the following questions honestly; there are no right or wrong answers here. When you have an idea of how you'll feel going through the sleep-training process, you'll feel better prepared and you'll feel more confident choosing a technique that will work for you and your child.

How do you feel when your child cries? Do you feel anxious? Frustrated? Worried? Normal?

_____

_____

_____

What do you feel you need to do when your child cries? Pick them up and soothe them? Help them without picking them up? Wait until you feel that they are asking for help before helping?

_____

_____

_____

How long are you going to be able to sleep train at the beginning of the night comfortably? Twenty minutes? An hour?

_____

_____

_____

Do you feel like you will need to give yourself a time-out? (A time-out is when you leave the room for a few minutes and go somewhere you can't hear your child. You can also wear your earbuds.)

_____

_____

_____

Establish a Routine Before Sleep Training

Routines come naturally to us. We usually get up around the same time each morning, eat at around the same time, and go to bed around the same time each night. The body's natural rhythms ensure that, even without a clock to go by, you do essentially the same things every day at about the same time.

Having a daily routine for your child does not need to be restrictive. You don't need to be home all day or never leave the house anywhere near naptime. What's important is that you have some sort of daily routine. You don't need to rush into a routine; you can spend a couple of weeks adjusting. This gives both you and your child a chance to adjust to your new normal.

How to Ease Into a Daily Routine

Start with the beginning of your day and work from there. Your child's wake-up time should be the same daily, even on those days when they seem to want to sleep in. I know the thought of waking a sleeping child is not what you had in mind, but it is beneficial in the long term. When your child sleeps an extra hour in the morning, it will have a domino effect on the rest of the day: The morning nap will be an hour late, the afternoon nap will be later, and, ultimately, so will bedtime.

Set a wake-up time that results in a reasonable bedtime. A normal amount of night sleep is usually between 10 and 12 hours. A 6:30 a.m. to 8:30 a.m. wake-up time means bedtime will be sometime between 6:30 p.m. and 8:30 p.m. Choose a bedtime that works for your family. This will be an important part of your daily routine, so try to maintain it consistently. If you follow the daily routine appropriate to your child's age, naptime will become more consistent and nap duration will be more predictable. And, by the way, it's okay to have a little wiggle room in your daily routine if it suits your family better; it doesn't have to be too regimented. Having a 30-minute window is usually okay.

Guidelines for Establishing a Routine

You know your child better than anybody, and you know how cranky they can get when they're overtired. If your child becomes grumpy when tired, you'll want to make sure you are following the daily routine pretty closely. If your child has a more intense/spirited or slow-to-warm-up temperament, you won't have much wiggle room before your child needs to nap or get to sleep for the night. On the other hand, laid-back and easygoing children have a much easier time handling a little bit of tiredness, and it won't impact the quality of their sleep. So, if your child is more laid-back, you can be a little less strict with the timings.

Set yourself up with a daily routine you can follow. If the routine you want to establish plans for your child to wake at 9:00 a.m., but they naturally rise at 7:00 a.m., you're already off the routine before you've started! If you set naptime close to the time you have to pick up your older child from school, you will have to wake your child from their nap. So, plan for naps when you know you won't need to be anywhere else for the usual duration of the nap. For example, if you always need to be out of the house at 1:00 p.m., you'll need your child to be awake before 1:00 p.m. Work your way back from this: They need to be awake at 12:45 p.m., which means they need to be asleep by 11:30 a.m. and need to be up from their first nap at 9:30 a.m.

Working around your daily schedule will set you up for success. The ideal daily routine will depend on your child's age; the older your child is, the easier time they will have remaining awake for longer periods. Take a look at the following routines and develop an age-appropriate routine for your child:

3 TO 4 MONTHS SAMPLE ROUTINE

1½ hours awake routine: A maximum awake period of an hour and a half is perfect for this age.

7:00 a.m.	Awake for the day
8:20 a.m.	Begin nap routine
8:30 a.m.	Work on falling asleep
9:30 a.m.	Awake from the nap
10:50 a.m.	Begin nap routine
11:00 a.m.	Work on falling asleep
11:30 a.m.	Awake from the nap
12:40 p.m.	Begin nap routine
12:50 p.m.	Work on falling asleep
2:30 p.m.	Awake from the nap
3:50 p.m.	Begin nap routine
4:00 p.m.	Work on falling asleep
5:00 p.m.	Awake from the nap
6:30 p.m.	Begin night routine

4½ TO 6 MONTHS SAMPLE ROUTINE

2 hours awake routine: A maximum awake period of two hours is perfect for this age. Naps may become a little more consistent, and your day may not feel so unpredictable.

7:00 a.m.	Awake for the day
8:50 a.m.	Begin nap routine
9:00 a.m.	Work on falling asleep
10:45 a.m.	Awake from the nap
12:30 p.m.	Begin nap routine
12:40 p.m.	Work on falling asleep
1:50 p.m.	Awake from the nap
3:40 p.m.	Begin nap routine
3:50 p.m.	Work on falling asleep
4:50 p.m.	Awake from the nap
6:30 p.m.	Begin night routine
7:30 p.m.	Work on falling asleep

6 MONTHS TO BETWEEN 15 AND 18 MONTHS SAMPLE ROUTINE

2, 3, 4 hours awake routine: The 2-3-4 routine works well for children over six months and who still take two naps a day. Your child is awake for two hours in the morning before going down for their first nap. They're then awake for three hours before taking their second nap. Then they're awake for four hours before going down for the night. With three hours total of day sleep, we have a 12-hour day. If the four-hour stretch is too long, you can add a catnap. This catnap should be just long enough to keep your child going until bedtime. Your child will no longer need the catnap once they reach seven and a half or eight months old.

7:00 a.m.	Awake for the day
8:50 a.m.	Begin nap routine
9:00 a.m.	Work on falling asleep
10:30 a.m.	Awake from the nap
1:20 p.m.	Begin nap routine
1:30 p.m.	Work on falling asleep
3:00 p.m.	Awake from the nap
6:30 p.m.	Begin night routine
7:00 p.m.	Work on falling asleep

BETWEEN 15 AND 18 MONTHS SAMPLE ROUTINE

One nap a day routine: Children who take one nap will take that nap in the middle of the day. There is no set time for this nap. You'll want to make sure your child is not overtired when you try to get them down to sleep. Don't keep them up too long and don't let them nap too near to bedtime. If your child doesn't have a long awake period between waking from their nap and going to sleep for the night, they will struggle to fall asleep at bedtime. Most children will need around five hours of awake time between waking from their nap and falling asleep at night.

7:00 a.m.	Awake for the day
12:30 p.m.	Begin nap routine
12:45 p.m.	Work on falling asleep
2:45 p.m.	Awake from nap
7:00 p.m.	Begin bedtime routine
7:45 p.m.	Asleep for the night

Consistency Is Key

You must be consistent. Understand the technique you have chosen and follow it to the letter. Don't give up or give in. Inconsistency isn't fair to your child. It's not fair to make your child feel frustrated (as sleep training almost inevitably does) and then give in after their frustration reaches a peak. It would be really annoying if it happened to you, and it makes sleep training take much longer than it should. You don't want your child to learn that the only way they can get what they want (you helping them to sleep) is to be frustrated for a very long time.

No one sleep-training technique is any better than any other. You'll know which technique is more likely to work for your child. When you use the right technique, consistency is what makes it effective.

Start Them Early . . . But Don't Stress If You Can't

As I've mentioned, there is no perfect age to begin sleep training. Yes, there are some ages and stages when it may be a little easier for your child, but as their parent, you'll know the right time to get started. Don't feel pressured into starting sleep training by your pediatrician, family members, friends, or random strangers. If you are happy with how your child is sleeping, there is nothing to change and you're doing great. It's only a problem when it's a problem. You (and your partner) will know when to get started.

There is a lot of conflicting advice on the best time to get started with sleep training. I have been working with families for over 20 years, and even I don't tell them the best time to begin sleep training. It's up to them. That's because I think it's best for parents to follow their instincts. The only parameter I have is: Wait until your child is ready.

I'm not averse to general guidelines, though, so you should find the following helpful: Laid-back and easygoing children can get started at four months with a gentle technique or at six months for Cry-It-Out. More intense/spirited and slow-to-warm-up children should wait until at least six months before getting started with a hands-on, gentle technique where you remain in the room as they are learning the new skills to get themselves to sleep. If your child is older than this, that's okay. There's no reason to stress. Just follow the instructions for your chosen technique.

Set Up a Calming, Comforting Sleep Environment

The American Academy of Pediatrics suggests room sharing with your child for the first 6 to 12 months. With this in mind, you will want to work on adapting your bedroom. For starters, keep the bedroom dark while your child is sleeping or getting ready for sleep (you can turn a lamp on if needed). We all sleep better in the dark. Installing blackout curtains or room-darkening blinds can keep outside light from brightening up the room.

Don't use a laptop, tablet, or phone in the bedroom during bedtime. The light that these screens emit prevents the production of melatonin, a natural hormone our bodies produce when we get into a dark space that induces sleep. Going to bed right after looking at a screen can lead to more restless sleep, so having some time away from the TV or your phone before bed can help you sleep better.

You'll also want to keep energy-saving light bulbs out of the bedroom as they also inhibit the production of melatonin. An incandescent bulb in a lamp is perfect for when you are getting your child ready for sleep.

Don't paint the nursery in bright colors or have too many busy, stimulating pictures in the room (the same goes for your bedroom if you are sharing the space), as these can make it harder for your child to relax before falling asleep. Sticking with muted colors, such as calm blues, earthy greens and browns, pale purples, and soft whites will help your baby relax.

White noise can be very relaxing for your child. The whooshing will remind them of being in the womb and lull them to sleep. Don't have the white-noise machine playing directly into your child's ears. The noise should fill the room, not blast your child. If your child doesn't seem to like white noise, or you don't like white noise, try brown or pink noise. Brown noise doesn't have any high-frequency sounds and, in pink noise, they are reduced. Brown or pink noise may be more pleasant for you and your child to listen to than white noise.

Prioritize Sleep Safety

You want to ensure your child is sleeping in a safe sleep space. The American Academy of Pediatrics suggests sharing a room for the first 6 to 12 months but not a bed with your child. Follow these guidelines (for children under 12 months) each time you put your child down to sleep to keep them safe:

○ Keep the room between 65°F and 70°F.

○ Your child's crib or bassinet mattress should be firm and meet the safety standard laid out by the US Consumer Product Safety Commission (CPSC).

○ Don't place the bassinet or crib next to a window.

○ Make sure there are no curtains or window blind pull cords near the crib.

○ The crib or bassinet should have a fitted sheet and nothing else. Bumpers, pillows, blankets, and stuffed animals are dangerous in the sleep space.

○ If you have a monitor, don't place this on the crib; it should be secured to the wall or placed on a separate surface.

○ Always place your child on their back to sleep. If your child can roll onto their stomach, they are okay to sleep there. You don't need to keep rolling them onto their backs.

○ If your child falls asleep in a swing, stroller, or car seat, move them to a safe flat surface as soon as possible.

○ Never place your baby on a sofa or chair to sleep.

EXERCISE: Baby Safety Checklist

Chances are you've taken many of these baby-safety precautions already. Spend a few moments running down this list and checking off all the precautions you've taken. If a box remains unchecked, put it on your to-do list.

☐ Cover open outlets

☐ Secure large pieces of furniture to the wall

☐ Secure and hide electrical cords

☐ Wrap up window blind cords

☐ Install baby gates at top and bottom of stairs

☐ Remove fridge magnets

☐ Remove chemicals from low cabinets

☐ Keep plastic bags out of low drawers

☐ Lock windows

☐ Place houseplants out of reach

☐ Use corner guards on furniture

☐ Install door guards to prevent trapping little fingers

☐ Keep toys within reach during playtime (not sleep time)

☐ Ensure that the crib or bassinet is free of bumpers, pillows, blankets, toys, and stuffed animals and placed away from a window and other hazards

☐ Remove a mobile when your child can sit up

☐ Keep diaper creams and similar items out of reach

Reducing the Risk of SIDS

Sudden infant death syndrome (SIDS) is the sudden and unexpected death of a child under 12 months of age. Though very little is known about SIDS and what causes it, we do know ways that SIDS can be significantly reduced. In addition to meeting the guidelines set forth earlier, you can also reduce the risk of SIDS by:

○ Breastfeeding or offering breast milk (as opposed to formula) in a bottle.

○ Allowing your child to use a pacifier during sleep.

○ Not smoking during or after pregnancy.

○ Vaccinating your child on the schedule recommended by your child's pediatrician.

○ Always placing your child on their back on a firm mattress in their own sleep space.

○ Keeping loose blankets out of your child's sleep space.

Responding to Other Health Issues

Some health issues can impact your child's sleep. Around 50 percent of babies will show some symptoms of reflux at least once a day before they are six months old, and 25 percent of babies show colic symptoms before they are three months old. Both reflux and colic can have a negative impact on your child's sleep, but there are things you can do to help your child feel more comfortable. Be sure to talk with your doctor if you think your child has reflux or colic.

REFLUX

Reflux is caused when the muscles at the top of the stomach are immature, and the contents of the stomach can come up into the esophagus. This causes discomfort as the stomach is full of acid. If you've ever had heartburn, you know how uncomfortable reflux can be. Some symptoms of reflux are:

○ Frequent spitting up, though not always; a child can have reflux without ever spitting up

○ Fussiness and crying when lying flat, especially after a feed

○ Sour breath

○ Gurgling in the esophagus when lying down

○ Wants to be held upright

○ Poor sleep during both naps and nighttime

Here are some tips for helping a child with reflux feel more comfortable:

○ Small feeds

○ Feeding your child at a 30-degree angle

○ Being held upright for 30 minutes after a feed

○ Wrapping a cummerbund around the tummy; the pressure can help your child feel more comfortable (make sure this isn't too tight; you want just a little pressure)

COLIC

Colic is frequent, prolonged periods of crying in a child under five months old. These periods of crying are usually in the evenings, can last up to three hours, and happen more than three days a week for at least three weeks. Up to 40 percent of infants have colic. Doctors are not sure what causes colic; some breastfeeding mothers find that eliminating certain foods (caffeine, dairy, soy, wheat, or eggs) from their diet can help their child become more comfortable. Here are some things you can try to help relieve colic:

○ Burping your child

○ Holding them in different positions

○ Music

○ White noise

○ Swaddling

○ Movement in a swing

EXERCISE: A Meditation Break

It's okay to give yourself a little time-out if you feel that you need it. Swap with your partner or, as long as your child is safe, it's fine to step away for a few minutes and go somewhere where you can't hear your child crying. If that's not possible, you can wear headphones.

1. Sit or lie down (a chair, bed, or floor is fine). Breathe in slowly through your nose and out through your mouth.

2. Slowly breathe in and out, in and out. Concentrate on your breathing, feeling your chest rise and fall and your belly grow and contract.

3. Ask yourself, "Why am I sleep training?" and "What skills are my child learning?"

4. Continue to breathe deeply. Ask yourself, "How will my nights be different when my child has learned these skills?" and "How will I feel when my child can get themselves to sleep?"

5. Remind yourself that you are in control. Acknowledge that this is tough, but it will get easier.

6. Take three more breaths in through your nose and out through your mouth. Slowly get up and continue with your sleep training.

Samantha's nine-month-old, Melody, could only fall asleep if she was being fed. This also meant that she couldn't get back to sleep at night without a feed. Samantha was exhausted and wanted to start sleep training. First, she worked on an age-appropriate daily routine, making sure that Melody was not getting overtired. Once Melody's day was more predictable, she had an easier time falling asleep at naptime and her naps increased from just 20 minutes to over an hour. This, in turn, had a positive impact on night sleep; she had a much easier time falling asleep at the beginning of the night and was sleeping for slightly longer stretches. With Melody sleeping a bit better, Samantha felt like she had enough energy to begin sleep training. Since Melody was having an easier time falling asleep, Samantha found that the process wasn't as challenging as she thought it would be. Soon, both mom and baby were getting better sleep.

The Role of Feedings

There is no magical age or weight when your child will no longer need to feed during the night. Yes, some children no longer need to night feed at 12 weeks, but most do. Feeding during the night is biologically normal for little humans. Some children are walking at 9 months while others are not walking until they are nearer to 18 months. We don't presume that because some children are walking at 9 months that all children can walk at that age. Think of no longer needing a feed during the night as another developmental stage.

Having said that, you don't have to feed *many* times throughout the night when you are sleep training, but you will want your child to have the minimum number of feeds each night. When your child has the skills to get themselves to sleep at the beginning of the night, they will also have the skills to get themselves to sleep during the night if they are not hungry.

At the beginning of the night, be sure you are not feeding your child to sleep or even getting them drowsy through feeding. You may want to feed your child at the very beginning of your bedtime routine, go through the steps in the routine, and then feed again at the end. Rather than feed your child to sleep, you will just be topping them off. They are not likely to fall asleep or get too drowsy with this little top off. Aim to put them in their crib relaxed but awake.

Decide how long you think your child can reasonably go between night feeds. If they have been feeding every three hours, stretching the feed to every four hours may be a great start. To cue your child that a feed is happening at night, turn on a night-light or a lamp (with an incandescent light bulb, which won't interfere with the production of melatonin). This tells your child that the light goes on for a feed, not just because they woke up.

When your child wakes, look at the time. Is it near to a feed time (within 15 minutes of your set time)? If so, turn the light on and feed your child, trying not to feed them to sleep. You can swap sides, remove the breast or bottle, talk, or tickle little feet to try to keep your child as awake as possible before putting them back into bed. If it is not a feed time, you will use your chosen sleep-training technique until they have fallen back asleep or you have bumped up to feed time, at which point you will turn on the light to signal to your child that it is time to feed.

You don't want night feeds to be too exciting and stimulating, so keep the lights dim, the room reasonably quiet, and try not to interact too much with your child. Night feeds should be all business.

Breastfeeding

Breastfeeding can be a little easier than bottle-feeding at night since there is nothing to prepare; you already have everything you need. Unfortunately, this means that night feeds are going to be the responsibility of the mom. If this is you, you can still have your partner help you with the night feed; they can be responsible for dealing with any diaper changes and bringing the baby to you while you make yourself comfortable.

Formula and Expressed Breast Milk

Night feeds can feel a little more unsettled if you're storing breast milk or formula feeding because you need to get that bottle ready. Make sure you have everything prepared before you go to bed so you can quickly warm up the bottle when your child wakes during the night. Follow the guidelines for mixing formula and leaving it out of the fridge once it has been heated.

Daytime and Nighttime Sleep Are Both Important

Daytime sleep and nighttime sleep complement each other, but they are not the same. As I mentioned earlier, night sleep begins to develop (lengthens and becomes more consistent) sometime between 6 and 12 weeks; naps can lag behind a little and don't start to develop until sometime between 4 and 6 months.

Chances are your child's naps and night sleep are vastly different experiences for both you and your child. For example, your 14-week-old may be beginning to get a longer stretch of sleep at the very beginning of the night but continues to nap for just 45 minutes. Or you may struggle more getting your child to sleep at bedtime than you do at naptime. Differences like these are quite normal.

Remember, if your child becomes overtired, they will struggle to fall asleep and remain asleep at naptime because their brain is just too stimulated. Come nighttime, whether they are overtired or undertired because they napped too close to bedtime, your child could have a tougher time falling asleep for the night and may wake more often. Following an age-appropriate daily routine (see page 54) will ensure that your child is neither lacking sleep nor getting too much sleep. In these routines, daytime and nighttime sleep are equally important for good sleep all around.

How Many Naps Are Too Many Naps?

The number of naps your child needs daily depends on your child's age. The younger your child, the more time they will spend napping. A four-month-old may need four or five naps a day, whereas a two-year-old will only need one nap a day. You do want to make sure your child isn't getting too much nap sleep throughout the day;

it should be enough to keep them going until the next naptime or bedtime. Refer back to the sample routines provided earlier to figure out the timing.

Change Is Hard, but Stay Positive

Human beings are creatures of habit. We like it when we know what will happen next, so change can be hard for us. When you first get started sleep training, acknowledge that this new experience can make both you and your child feel uncertain and frustrated. Also be aware that sleep may become a little trickier before it gets better. This is because your child is breaking the habit of relying on you and learning the skills they need to rely on themselves. This takes time. There is no quick fix when it comes to sleep. It might feel like you're just plodding along, but that's okay. Every child learns at their own pace; some more slowly than others. The speed doesn't matter. Your goal remains the same: better sleep for your whole family. This process will get easier for you and your child, so just keep moving forward.

Conclusion

When you prepare for sleep training, you'll feel more confident carrying out the technique you have chosen. When you feel confident, your child will sense that and feel more relaxed. When you (and your partner) feel confident and calm when sleep training begins, you can move through the steps with more ease, which makes sleep training much easier for your family. Don't skip these preparations; they may not seem significant when it comes to teaching independent sleep skills, but they create a solid foundation from which to proceed.

Chapter 4

Baby's New Nightly Sleep Routine

ROUTINES HELP YOUR CHILD RELAX, AND A relaxed child will have an easier time falling asleep. Once your child is relaxed, you can pop them into bed and use your sleep-training technique to help them get to sleep. In this chapter, I share some of the best routines to help your child fall asleep more readily. You'll learn to determine when to soothe your child and the best way to do so. You'll also learn to manage wake-ups, reduce night feeds, and remain consistent so you can see progress as quickly as possible.

Create a Sleep Log

Use a sleep log to keep track of when your child is sleeping. A sleep log isn't just for when you start sleep training. Lots of families like to track their child's natural sleep rhythms using a log or diary. You can create a spreadsheet on your computer and print it out. Use this sample log as a template. This template is for one day.

DATE:	TIME
Awake for the day:	
Started nap routine:	
Asleep for nap:	
Awake from nap:	
Started nap routine:	
Asleep for nap:	
Awake from nap:	
Started nap routine:	
Asleep for nap:	
Awake from nap:	
Started night routine:	
Asleep for the night:	
Night waking (one time awake):	
Back asleep:	
Night waking (two times awake):	
Back asleep:	
Night waking (three times awake):	
Back asleep:	
Additional wake-ups:	

The Benefits of Keeping a Sleep Log

A sleep log can help you identify patterns in your child's sleep. If your child takes a short nap, you can review your log to see if their awake time was too long or maybe too short. If your child seems overstimulated while you are getting them ready for their nap, you can look back and see if perhaps a nap earlier in the day, an awake period, or a timing issue caused the problem.

You might notice that your child falls into a similar pattern with their wake-ups, as children often do. Do they get a long stretch of sleep at the beginning of the night? Is their first nap of the day always longer than subsequent ones? With a log, you'll be able to answer these questions and more. The more predictable your child's sleep becomes, the easier time you will have working with their natural sleep rhythm.

A log is also an excellent way to track your sleep-training progress once you've started the process. You can see (and celebrate!) when your child is sleeping for longer stretches, when they drop night feeds, and when they fall back to sleep with ease.

When and How to Start a Sleep Log

I encourage you to keep a sleep log for at least a week before you begin making changes with sleep. You can take a look at the information you've collected and gradually make changes to your child's sleep schedule as needed. You'll also be able to track any subsequent changes with how they are sleeping.

I provided a sample template earlier, but there are many different smartphone apps that help you keep track not only of sleep but also of diaper changes and feeds. My preference is paper and pencil to track sleep. Using a printout of the template, you'll jot down the times you began the nap or night routine, when you started helping your child to sleep, what time they fell asleep, and what time they awoke, as well as the duration of long night wakings. If an app works better for you, be sure it follows a structure that's similar to the template.

Commit to Your Technique

Whenever you get started with sleep training, you want to continue your chosen method for at least a week before deciding if the technique is working for your child. Remember, you and your child are breaking habits and learning new skills, and that is not something that happens instantly. Most families begin to see progress on night three or four, but you may see results sooner or maybe a little later. Though you want your child to be sleeping independently as quickly as possible, be prepared to spend at least a week working on it. Many parents report that sleep training is going well at the one-week mark.

Make sure you know your technique. You'll want to be on autopilot doing what you need to do when you need to do it. Don't start if you aren't sure what you need to be doing or when. If you haven't yet decided on one of the methods, return to chapter 2 and make your decision, but take your time doing so. As you go through the motions, you'll gain more expertise and confidence, and your child will sense this and feel more confident with you. If you're wondering what you need to be doing, your child will pick up on that uncertainty and have a harder time relaxing. So once you choose which technique you will be using, know it inside and out.

Establish a Peaceful Place to Sleep

It's true for all of us: The more relaxed we are before we try to fall asleep, the easier time we have falling asleep. To help relax your child, keep their bedroom tidy and clutter-free. Not only is a tidy environment more relaxing for you and your child, but it is also safer. You may be navigating your child's bedroom in the dark when you're not fully awake, so make sure the path from the door to the crib presents no tripping hazards. The same is true if you are sharing a bedroom with your child. If you feel relaxed and calm and you begin to yawn during your child's night routine, the space is perfect.

Quiet Room

Keep the bedroom relatively quiet while you are helping your child get ready for sleep. This will help them relax. You can play relaxing music as you go through your routine. The more relaxed your child is through the routine, the easier time they'll have falling asleep.

Don't feel that you need to tiptoe around while your child is sleeping or while you are trying to get them to sleep; a little bit of ambient noise is okay and may not disturb your child. However, they are likely to be disturbed by a sudden big noise such as a dog barking or a loud sibling.

Remember, every child is unique. Some children will have an easy time sleeping through noise, and others will struggle. If your child struggles to sleep through household noises, you may want to try playing white, pink, or brown noise in the bedroom.

Crib

In chapter 3, we discussed creating a safe sleep space for your child, including making sure the crib is clutter-free. Remember, you want to keep the crib as minimal as possible for safety's sake. The crib should be free of loose blankets, so if your child does need a blanket, make sure it is tucked in. A wearable blanket or sleep sack is perfect for children under 12 months. Keep toys out of the crib when your child is there to sleep; you want them to be working on sleeping, not playing. If you plan to have a mobile on the side of the crib, you may want to get one that can easily be removed at the end of the day so that your child isn't so stimulated by it that they can't sleep.

You certainly want the crib to be a safe space, but that doesn't mean the crib can't be an inviting space. It can be far from relaxing to get into a cold bed at the beginning of the night. To remedy this, you can place a hot water bottle or heating pad on the lowest setting in the crib for a few minutes before you place your child into bed.

Important: *If you warm up your child's bed with a water bottle or heating pad, you must remember to remove the item before you place your child into bed. Never leave a heating pad, hot water bottle, or any other device in the crib with your child.*

Another way to help your child feel more relaxed and comforted in their crib is to use a crib sheet that has your smell. You can do this by placing a clean crib sheet on your bed for a few hours before fitting it over their mattress. The scent of you can help your child feel more secure.

The Great Debate:
Bed Sharing versus Crib

As I mentioned earlier, the American Academy of Pediatrics suggests sharing a room for the first 6 to 12 months but not a bed with your child. Ultimately, the decision to bed share or not is up to you *and* your partner. You both need to be fully on board with bed sharing and must ensure that the sleep space is safe. If you are waking during the night and bringing your child to your bed for a feeding, you will still want to make sure that the space is safe for your child, just in case you fall back asleep. If you are nursing while lying down, make sure your child is between you and a wall or bedrail, not between you and your partner. There should be no gap between the mattress and the headboard, bedrail, or wall. Make sure there are no pillows, blankets, or comforters near your child. Keep long hair tied back, and don't wear anything that has loose ties.

When I started working with Kelly, her 11-month-old, James, needed to be rocked to sleep at the beginning of the night. He was waking multiple times a night and would only fall back asleep when being rocked. We started working on the 2-3-4 routine (see page 55), and James almost instantly had an easier time napping and didn't require as much rocking to sleep at the beginning of the night.

Kelly started sleep training James on a Friday evening. He fell asleep within 30 minutes without being rocked. When James woke throughout the night, Kelly used the sleep-training technique she'd chosen, and James fell back asleep without rocking for each of his wake-ups. Night two was a little more challenging, as is often the case when it comes to changing sleep habits, and it took James 50 minutes to fall asleep at the beginning of the night with roughly the same number of night wakings. On night three, however, Kelly saw a significant improvement: James fell asleep within 15 minutes and only woke twice. Over the next week, James continued to improve, eliminating all the night wake-ups. Kelly was delighted.

Bedtime Routine

If your child goes straight from playing to bed, they won't be as relaxed and will have a harder time falling asleep. A bedtime routine can help your child transition from play to sleep. If you don't already have a consistent bedtime routine in place, start your routine at least a week before you begin sleep training.

Your bedtime routine should be consistent; when the routine is consistent, your child can predict what is coming next, and when they know what's coming next, they are more relaxed. This consistency will also mean that your child knows that sleep is coming, and they will begin to get ready to fall asleep as you are going through the predictable steps of the routine.

Do the bedtime routine in the same place and in the same order. Many families start their bedtime routine with a bath. However, if you don't bathe your child every evening, your routine will begin after a bath. Dress your child in their diaper and pajamas. A massage before dressing can be a wonderful way to help your child relax. You may have some quiet play (no rough and tumble here, please), time to read a book or two and/or sing a few songs, and then work on getting to sleep.

Your bedtime routine should be between 30 and 45 minutes. Don't miss out on steps of this routine if your child seems overtired; make each step a little shorter if you need to. That way, your routine stays consistent and predictable, you are not rushing through, and your child can fall asleep a little earlier.

Get Your Child (and Yourself) Settled

Starting sleep training may make you feel a little anxious, and that's completely understandable. When you're ready to start, use your bedtime routine as a way of calming, relaxing, and settling your child before they get into bed. But also try to relax yourself as much as possible during the routine. If you are feeling anxious, your child will pick up on that and they will have a harder time settling down. The more relaxed you are, the more comfortable your child will be. You can try any of the relaxation exercises included in this book to help calm you before you begin the bedtime routine. Let's look at a few other ways to settle your child down.

ROCKING CHAIR

Lots of families have a rocking chair in the nursery. Families have been using them for hundreds of years as ways to soothe, calm, and relax babies, and for a good reason. Rocking back and forth is more relaxing and calming than side-to-side motion. You can use a rocking chair as part of your bedtime routine as well as your nap routine; it's also the perfect spot to read to your child. Just make sure they don't get too drowsy or fall asleep while in the chair.

SOOTHING MUSIC

What better way to relax when getting ready for sleep and falling asleep than with some soothing music? Be mindful of the music you are using to soothe your child; though classical music may seem to be a good fit, it can get loud and energetic. The music you would hear playing in a spa is perfect. A Bluetooth speaker, which you can control from your phone, can be a helpful way to play music at a reasonable volume in your baby's bedroom. It's okay to play the music during the routine and while your child sleeps if you find that helps. When my now-teenagers were little, I had to cart around my CD player and CDs! Fortunately, with today's technology, it's easy to have some music playing to relax your child.

COOS, SHUSHES, AND SOOTHING

Use your voice to soothe your child during the bedtime routine (as well as when you are in the room with them during wake-ups). Your voice can be very relaxing for your child.

If your child is crying, don't talk over them to be heard; that will quickly turn into a shouting match. Quietly talk, sing, or shush. If you can't think of anything to say that you feel will be soothing and relaxing, don't worry, just talk. You can give a running commentary of how you both are feeling: "I can see you're so frustrated right now. I know you want me to pick you up and rock you to sleep. I'm right here for you. I can see that this is tough for you; it's also tough for me. Just think about how great this will be when you get yourself to sleep easily." If you feel the need to sing, you don't have to sing lullabies. Sing your favorite song, and don't worry about what you sound like. Remember, your child thinks you have the most fantastic singing voice.

If you are holding your child to soothe them, you can rock (back and forth is more relaxing than side to side), walk around the room, hold them while sitting on a yoga ball and bounce, or even do squats while holding them (but, admittedly, working out is not so fun in the middle of sleep training). When you are holding your child to soothe them (whether this is in the midst of sleep training or during the bedtime routine), remain in your child's room. You don't want your child thinking that the bedtime routine or sleep training has stopped.

Sleep Training Begins

Once you've completed your bedtime routine, that's when it's time to start using the technique you've chosen. You can do this! Some things you do will remain consistent no matter which sleep-training method you are using.

Put Baby in the Crib While They Are Awake

You will always want to put your child into their crib while they are still awake. Don't aim for drowsy; you want them to get into bed relaxed but awake. You may have been advised to aim for drowsy but awake, but I don't think this helps in the long term. Imagine how you would feel if you were moved just as you were falling asleep? I would be instantly awake and furious, so I understand why the drowsy-but-awake method fails for so many children. If your child can fall asleep from wide-awake at the beginning of the night, then when they naturally wake during the night (remember, this can happen up to six times a night), they can get themselves back to sleep. They won't need you to help them get drowsy first.

Say a Few Words of Comfort/ Encouragement/Love

Talk to your child as you place them into their crib and continue to talk for a little after you have laid them down. Explain to your child what you are doing and why. Let them know that you love them and you will be there for them, as well as how great it will be for them when they can quickly get themselves to sleep and back to sleep during the night. These encouraging words are just as vital for you as they are for your child, and they can help you feel a little more relaxed.

Tips for Calming Your Baby

Sometimes your child may get themselves into a bit of a pickle and just can't seem to stop crying and get calm. Here are some tips you may find helpful:
- Rocking back and forth
- Rocking side to side
- Loud "shushes" (not into your child's ears)
- Patting the back (nonrhythmically, if possible)
- Walking around the room
- Bouncing on a yoga ball/doing lunges while holding your baby
- Singing
- Big swings in your arms

You may find that stopping and starting the support you give is a little reminder to your child that you are trying to help and soothe them.

Leave the Room

Regardless of the sleep-training technique you are using, if your child is okay in the crib, you can step away and leave the room. Remember, you can always return if needed. Cry-It-Out does require you to leave the room for your preset time. If you're using one of the other sleep-training techniques, it's okay to remain in the room if that's what you are comfortable doing.

To Check or Not to Check

When to check on your child depends on the sleep-training technique you are using. If you are using Cry-It-Out, you will need to stick with your timed checks. If you are using any of the other sleep-training techniques, you can go back into the room when you feel your child is asking for help—not when the cry is fussy and whiny, but when the cry feels a little more urgent.

Different Methods for Checking In

If you are using Cry-It-Out, keep your checks to a minimum. You will not be picking up your child to soothe them, but you can enter the room and talk to them to comfort. You can also be hands-on and touch them if you think that will be helpful, but you cannot pick them up. After a few minutes, leave the room.

With Pat-the-Baby and Tippy-Toe-Out, you can pick up your child when the cry becomes more urgent. Pick them up to soothe and then place them back down. If they are content, you can leave the room again.

With the Michi method, you can pick your child up whenever you feel they are asking for help—not at the fussy-whiny cry, but the urgent cry that needs a little help. You can soothe your child by walking, rocking, bouncing, and dancing—just not feeding. When they have soothed, pop them back into bed. If they are content, you can leave the room. Most parents remain in the bedroom once they have gone back in, but some plan on not leaving the room at all.

Your Planned Response

By now it should be clear that your plan of action will depend on the sleep-training technique you are using. If you are using Cry-It-Out, you will be going to your child at set intervals, regardless of how hard they are crying. The other, more hands-on techniques let you remain in the bedroom to help your child when you feel that they need help. (If you're not clear about how to respond, review the technique again until you know it inside and out.)

Always remember that you know your child better than anyone; you know how they sound when they are asking for help. As mentioned earlier, an urgent cry is not to be confused with the fussy or whiny cry, which is not a sign your child is asking for help. When they are asking for help, the cry becomes urgent. An urgent cry will feel different to you; your instinct will kick in to help your child. It's the cry that makes you jump out of bed before you've even woken up or the cry that makes you drop everything to go and help. It just sounds different. When this cry happens, you can help your child by being hands-on, soothing with rubs or gentle pats, or even picking up your child if they need a little more support.

Pull Back on Nighttime Feedings

If you have been feeding your child during the night, it's a good idea to continue to feed them initially, setting the time between the feeds and using the night-light or lamp as a cue for a feed. When habits have been broken and new skills are learned, it's a good idea to see if you can tweak your feeds and begin lengthening the time between them. There are a few different techniques you can use when working on reducing night feeds, as follows:

Option 1: Once your child has the skills to get themselves to sleep, give them plenty of opportunity to get themselves back to sleep even if they wake for one of your scheduled feed times. You never know, they may be able to get themselves back to sleep without your needing to go in and feed. Try this starting with night four of sleep training.

Option 2: Stretch the time out between night feeds. If you have been feeding every four hours throughout the night, increase the time between the feeds to four and a half or five hours. You can use your sleep-training technique to help you get to your new feed time. Your child may fall back asleep without needing to feed. Stretch the time a little longer every other night of sleep training.

Option 3: Reduce the amount you are feeding. At your scheduled feed time, give your child a little less milk or formula. The reduction will help your child's stomach adjust to smaller feeds as the nights go by. Reduce bottle feedings by an ounce and breastfeeding by a minute or two, as this small reduction will be barely noticeable to your child. You can try this with all your night feedings at once or work on one at a time. Reduce another ounce or a few minutes of nursing every other night.

Phase Out Naps

As your child grows and develops, their daily sleep needs will change. Your child will be able to go longer between their naps, and they will reduce the number of naps they take each day.

In chapter 3, I shared with you the ideal daily routines for all ages. You can see in those examples how your child's day changes: They move from taking three or more naps a day to just two naps, then to one, and finally dropping that last nap. It's easy to shift from three or more naps a day down to two simply by lengthening the time between your child's naps. However, it get a little trickier when you drop from two naps to just one nap a day.

If you see one or more of the following signs for at least three or more consecutive days and your child is between 12 and 18 months, they are likely ready to transition to one nap:

○ Having a harder time falling asleep for either of their naps (though this usually occurs with the second nap of the day).

○ Taking shorter naps (this is more likely to occur with the first nap of the day).

○ Doesn't seem to be as tired at the beginning of the night and has a harder time falling asleep.

○ Beginning to wake earlier in the morning.

Here's the easiest way I know to make the transition:

1. Make morning naptime 30 to 45 minutes later than usual. Once asleep, let them nap as long as they want.

2. Make the second awake period around 30 minutes longer than usual. A second nap shouldn't be too long; it needs to be just long enough to keep your child's bedtime consistent. The longer this nap is, the later bedtime will be. Don't be afraid to wake your child from this second nap so you can keep the last awake period of the day around four hours.

3. Shift the morning nap 15 to 30 minutes later every third day. Continue to keep the awake time between naps one and two consistent. Remember, you may need to wake them to keep the last awake period of the day around four hours.

4. Keep shifting the morning nap until it is around lunchtime; then you can stop the second nap. It shouldn't be too hard to drop as it would have been quite short. It's okay to make the nightly bedtime a little earlier for a few days if your child is very tired after dropping the catnap.

Your child will eliminate their nap sometime between three and five years. The signs they are ready to begin the process are the same as when they are ready to reduce to one nap—having a hard time falling asleep for their nap, a harder time falling asleep at the beginning of the night, and beginning to wake earlier in the morning.

At this point, don't change the time that the nap is happening; rather, slightly reduce the amount they are sleeping. That means waking your child. Start by waking them from the nap about 20 minutes earlier than they'd usually wake up. Do the same for a week and see how their sleep is going: Are they beginning to have an easier time falling asleep at the beginning of the night? Are they sleeping later in the morning? If the reduction in the nap has not resolved the difficulties of falling asleep or the morning wake-up, reduce the nap a little more, again waking your child if you need to.

Continue to reduce the naptime, waiting a week to see if you need to make any additional reduction in nap duration. Often, a decrease in nap duration will help your child get back on track with nights and mornings. When the nap is short (20 minutes or so) and you are unable to reduce any more, this is the perfect time to drop the nap altogether.

How to Standardize a Nap Schedule

In chapter 3, I shared with you the perfect daily routine for your child's age. These are not set in stone, of course, because you are working with a unique individual. These are guidelines and give you a rough idea of how long your child should be awake before going down for their naps. Nap duration will be different for every child. I believe any nap over an hour is a good nap.

Tips for Multiples

With multiples (twins or more), you are working with different personalities, likely with quite different sleep habits. They will probably share a bedroom, but if you were thinking of keeping them in separate rooms so they don't disturb one another and plan for them to share a room in the future, it will probably be easier to start now—especially if one is a noisy sleeper, as this will give the other(s) time to adjust. Placing a white noise machine between the cribs can help block out a little sound if one child wakes and needs some help.

Know, too, that each child will have a way they prefer to be comforted; for example, one may prefer to be sung to and the other rocked. Be consistent with the way you support each one.

If one child wakes up for a night feed, some parents wake the other child/children and feed them, too. Doing this helps keep the multiples on a similar schedule, which means you can get more sleep.

Nap Routine

A nap routine should take about 10 to 15 minutes and have at least three steps performed in a consistent order. What does a nap routine look like? Here is an example:

1. Diaper change and get into a sleep sack.

2. Close curtains and turn on a lamp.

3. Read a book or two (ending story time with the same book) or singing songs (ending song time with the same song).

4. Feed.

Nap Routine Steps

Write down the steps of your child's nap routine below.

1. _____

2. _____

3. _____

4. _____

5. _____

Bedtime Routine

A bedtime routine should take about 30 to 45 minutes and have at least five steps performed in a consistent order. What does a bedtime routine look like? Here is an example:

1. Bath/massage and pajamas on.

2. Playtime with some quiet toys.

3. Get into a sleep sack.

4. Close curtains and turn on a lamp.

5. Read a book or two (ending story time with the same book) or singing songs (ending song time with the same song).

6. Feed.

Bedtime Routine Steps

Write down the steps of your child's bedtime routine below.

1. _____

2. _____

3. _____

4. _____

5. _____

6. _____

Be Patient and Track Your Progress

Regardless of the sleep-training technique you are using, it will take time for you to see results. Remember, you are in this for the long haul. In time, your child will sleep more independently, and they will have an easier time sleeping. Each night you sleep train, your child is learning the skills they need to sleep better.

To keep track of your progress, take a look at your sleep log each day. Note the improvements your child is making as well as new patterns that are emerging. When you're in the thick of sleep training, it can feel like you're not making much progress, but your sleep log will have a different story. You will see the step-by-step progress you and your child are making. You'll see them improve at the beginning of the night, how much longer they are sleeping, and a reduction in night feedings/wake-ups. Most families will begin to see improvements on nights three or four. Hang in there. I promise this will get easier.

Conclusion

Getting started sleep training is the hardest part, and now that you're underway, you have taken a giant leap toward better sleep for your whole family. Congratulations! With that said, life will inevitably throw you curveballs, so you'll want to be prepared. In the next chapter, I'll help you continue to make progress, even in the face of unexpected circumstances as well as those you might encounter as a matter of course in daily life.

Chapter 5
Stick with It

AS HARD AS THAT INITIAL SLEEP TRAINING IS, when it comes to having your child sleep more independently, sticking with that training is even harder. When you start sleep training, you are motivated and excited to begin. Once you start to see results and your child is having an easier time sleeping, you revel in the success, and rightly so. You may think all the hard work is done. But to continue with better sleep, you must remain consistent and stick with the routines you put into place. If you let your routines slide, your child's sleep habits will also slide, and you may end up back at square one. In this chapter, I'll show you how to navigate these ups and downs and continue with great sleep.

The Hardest Part Is Doing It Day after Day

Now that you've perfected your daily nap and bedtime routines and your child is getting better sleep, you don't want to backtrack and let sleep become a challenge again. For sleep to remain consistent, you need your routines to stay consistent. If you begin changing these routines now, you may start to see more wake-ups through the night, and your child may struggle to fall asleep at the beginning of the night.

Don't mess with those routines, no matter how tempting it is. Sometimes families contact me after we've spent weeks working together, saying their child is no longer sleeping well at night. They admit that they have let their daily routine slip a little, they're not so strict with timings, and the consequence is their night sleep is beginning to suffer. I don't want this to happen to you: You've put all the hard work into sleep training! Don't lose all the progress you've made by getting slack with your routines.

Unforeseen Events and Interruptions

Every family runs into changes that upset the daily routine and make sleep hard to come by. Many of these changes will not cause long-term sleep issues, and you'll be back on track within a few days. Other events will have a long-term impact on how your child is sleeping, and your child may not bounce back so quickly. The general rule of thumb here is, the longer your child is out of good habits, the longer it will take them to get back into good habits. If your child is bothered by teething for one or two nights and they need more support through the night due to their being in pain, they should bounce back to better sleep when they are no longer in pain. By contrast, if your child was sick for six or seven days and they needed more help and support through the night, it will take them a few more nights to get back on track.

When you are working on getting back on track with sleep, you will want to restart your sleep training. Don't worry, it won't be as tricky as it was when you first got started; it's more of a nudge in the right direction for your child.

Travel

Imagine travel from the small child's perspective: Suddenly the family packs up, gets into the car or on an airplane, straps them in the car seat for hours on end, and finally winds up in a strange place, with strange beds, strange people, and strange smells. From your child's point of view, everything familiar is gone.

Travel is difficult for adults, too, making them short-tempered and anxious. Add a little jet lag, and you may wonder why you decided to take your trip in the first place. Luckily, there are things you can do to make travel as easy as possible for your family while you are traveling.

As much as possible, stick to your daily routine. Jet lag may disorder your sleep for a few days, but children have a much easier time than adults when it comes to adapting their sleep schedule. Make sure you stick to your usual daily routine. Having changed your sleep schedule to local time, that may mean starting your day earlier than you would at home or staying up later than you usually would. Don't skip naps, especially during the first few days at your destination. Stick with your nap and bedtime routines; though the venue is different and your child is sleeping somewhere new, a familiar routine will help your child fall asleep a little easier.

If you are taking a travel crib with you for your child to sleep in, you can have some practice naps at home before you travel. This allows your child to get comfortable with the new sleep space before your trip. You can even pop your crib sheet from your child's crib (assuming it fits securely on the travel crib mattress) and the pajamas they wore the night before your trip in a zipper storage bag. They will smell of home, and that familiar scent can be very relaxing.

Tips for Keeping Baby on Schedule During Travel

Continue with your morning waking time, even when traveling. The thought of sleeping in does sound wonderful when you're on vacation, but having an inconsistent wake time will lead to inconsistent naps and an irregular bedtime. Too much wiggle room will be confusing to your child; they will miss out on sleep, and they will become tired and grumpy. Here are additional tips to keep in mind:

Plan your day. You can move your naps around a little if you need to be doing something at a particular time, but if you need to go out right in the middle of naptime, chances are your child will not go back to sleep once you have woken them. In this case, start your nap a little earlier so they have had a good nap before you need to wake them.

Sleep may get disrupted. When you travel, it can take a little while to become comfortable with a different environment and a change from our regular routines. This can result in sleep disturbances. Your child may need a bit more help getting to sleep, and you may have renewed night wakings. Don't panic; it's quite normal.

Know ahead of time where your child will sleep. Are you taking a travel crib with you? Does your destination have a crib? Again, if you are taking a travel crib, have your child take some practice naps in it before you leave so it doesn't feel so new.

Try to stick to the same feed schedule. Feed your child based on your home time zone. You can gradually shift to earlier or later to get onto your new time zone if you will be away long enough to make this necessary. This shift should not be done too quickly since you will be going longer stretches without food or trying to feed too soon.

Hold off and soothe. If your child wakes more often during the night, don't feed them the second they wake, unless, of course, you are confident they are hungry. Try soothing other ways before feeding; placing a hand on their tummy may be all they need. You can try picking them up for a hug, rocking them a little, or singing a song. Increase help if you need to, and don't be afraid to feed your child if you think your child needs it.

You may need to be comfortable with some level of sleep disruption while you're away from home, but the more you can maintain your usual routine, the better.

Overnight Guests

Having visitors stay with you shouldn't be as disruptive as traveling, but you may feel that it is impacting your child's sleep. Well-meaning family and friends can be very overstimulating for your little one, and the more overstimulated they are, the harder it will be for them to fall asleep and remain asleep. Your child's brain is overloaded, and it can't shut off as quickly. Protect your child's daily routine and try to stick to their nap schedule.

It's not always going to be possible to take every nap at home if you are out and about with your guests, but do try to preserve at least one of your daily naps. It's usually easier to take the first nap at home. You'll also want to protect your child's bedtime. Having one or two late nights when you have guests is okay, but too many late nights are going to hurt your child's sleep. Unfortunately, they won't just sleep later in the morning; they will often just miss out on that sleep, making them more tired and grumpy. This tiredness can have a negative impact on how your child naps. When they are so tired, they can struggle to fall asleep and remain asleep, and the cycle of being tired and cranky continues.

Childcare

Often when you have a child in childcare, sleep is out of your control. It's not up to the parents when their child goes down for their nap. Childcare centers can be very stimulating and noisy places, and that can make it harder for your child to unwind and relax enough to get a good nap.

Don't hesitate to ask your childcare provider to follow your daily routine; they want your child to nap as well as you do. A child who has moved from an infant room to a toddler room (usually around their first birthday) may only be able to nap once a day. If this is the case, your child may be missing out on some sleep and may have a hard time remaining awake when they are picked up because they are so tired. This can lead to a "danger nap" on the way home. A danger nap is when a nap happens a little too close to bedtime, likely pushing bedtime later than you would like. Some ideas for avoiding this danger nap on the ride home is to play music, have a sing-along, talk with your child, and keep the windows open slightly to let in cool air.

Navigating Changes to the Family Structure

You know that life will be different when you add another person into the fold. If this is your first child, you (and your partner) will get to your new normal day by day. If you have other children, be aware that bringing a new baby home can be tough on them. Your baby's older sibling may feel like their whole way of life has been turned upside down. Luckily, this time of transition is pretty short-lived. I'll discuss involving your older child in the baby's routine in just a moment, but here are two other ways to help older siblings adjust to the new addition to your family:

○ If you need to transition an older sibling out of a crib so the baby can sleep there, do this sooner rather than later. You don't want your older child feeling like they had to give up their bed so that the baby can sleep there. Transition your older child at least two months before the baby arrives so they can feel comfortable in their new bed.

○ Keep your older children's routines as consistent as possible. A predictable schedule will help your child feel more secure. If you need to adjust your child's routines before the baby arrives (maybe your partner is going to do the night routine), try to do this a couple of months before the baby arrives so your child does not feel that you are no longer able to help them get ready for bed. You don't want them to resent the baby.

Aside from bringing your new baby home and helping older children adjust, you may be faced with other changes to the family structure. Various events can take a parent away from home, including a business trip, a military deployment, or a hospital stay. More catastrophic events like death, incarceration, or marital separation trigger not only the removal of a parent from the home but a cascade of financial and emotional fallout that can complicate things. Remember, children can pick up on our psychological state, and any uncertainty on our part will contribute to their anxiety. Anxiety of any sort can interfere with sleep. Even as part of the most benign events, the fact that one parent is missing from the home can cause problems with sleep. The change can trigger separation anxiety and clinginess, as well as difficulty falling asleep and remaining asleep.

If your family structure has changed temporarily or permanently, remain as consistent as possible with established routines to give your child/children some stability and consistency. This will hopefully help them feel a little more secure. If your child is waking more or seems to need more support as they are falling asleep or going back to sleep due to these changes, go ahead and offer them the extra help they need, but try not to help too much. For instance, start with a tummy rub, but if that's still not helping, you can sing or talk as well. If that's not helping, you can pick them up, rock them, and so on, adding more support as needed. Don't swoop in and pick your child up and rock them into a deep sleep as soon as they begin to stir. Overhelping can quickly become a new habit that is much harder to break.

Involving an Older Sibling in Your Routine

Of course, you are only able to be in one place at one time; parents never feel this more than when they are helping a younger sibling sleep. As you are getting your little one ready for sleep, going through your wonderful routine and then helping them into bed, their older siblings are up to who knows what! Often, parents will rush through the routine, not wanting to leave an older child for too long. A nap

Megan wasn't sure how she would manage sleep training her seven-month-old at naptime, being by herself at home with the baby and her four-year-old daughter, Olivia. I suggested she begin nap training on a weekend when her partner was home and could take care of Olivia. We then developed a consistent nap routine for Megan to do with both the children. The routine took place in Olivia's bedroom. Olivia chose the books they would read and helped get her baby sister into her sleep sack. Megan would then leave Olivia in her bedroom to play with some toys while she helped the baby to sleep. The routine worked well. Olivia felt like an essential part of the family because she had important jobs to do to help with the baby. Megan felt great about the routine; she was able to give everyone the time they needed. She didn't feel like either of her children was deprived of precious time with Mom.

routine needs to be around 10 or 15 minutes long, and a toddler can get up to a lot of mischief in that time.

There are ways to make this work without having to worry about what your older child is up to. Have your older child take part in the routines. A bedtime routine does not require all of your children to go to sleep. You could do the routine in your older child's bedroom or even your bedroom. Before you begin your routine, make sure the room your baby will be sleeping in is all ready, curtains closed, white noise on, etc. Your older child can pick out the books you are going to read to your little one, and they can even read or make up a story or two as part of your winding down. Your older child can help with the diaper change or pass you the swaddle or sleep sack. Don't worry too much if they don't want to be very involved; you can go through the steps of the routine with your child in the room without needing them to participate. You will only need to leave them alone when you put the baby into their crib.

Adapting Your Daily Routine to Your Growing, Changing Baby

As your child grows, so do their sleep requirements. They will be able to stay awake for longer periods throughout the day, and you may need to help them make this adjustment. Some signs your child is ready for longer awake periods are:

○ **Struggling to fall asleep at naptime.** They may seem more awake and alert. This shouldn't be confused with being over-tired; an overtired child will also struggle to fall asleep. An overtired child may have a sudden burst of energy after they were showing you some tired signs (yawning, rubbing eyes, etc.). An overtired child will be fussier than an undertired child.

○ **Nap length reducing.** If your child was taking one-and-a-half hour naps and they suddenly reduce down to 45 minutes, your child may be ready for a longer awake period.

In chapter 3, I shared with you examples of different daily routines for different ages. If your child has spent a minimum of three consecutive days showing you signs they are ready for more extended awake periods, you'll know it's not just a temporary change. Gradually work on extending the time between the naps; don't try to do it one big jump, as that can often result in your child becoming overtired. Stretch out the awake periods by 15 to 20 minutes every third or fourth day. Taking this transition nice and slow will ensure your child gets back on track with their naps as quickly as possible.

Changes through the Stages up to 18 Months

It's relatively easy to adjust your child's daily routine when shifting from the one-and-a-half-hour routine to the two-hour routine and then to the 2-3-4 routine. You're slowly increasing those awake times. It can be a little trickier moving from the 2-3-4 routine to one nap, as you'll need to drop one of those naps altogether.

Start by increasing the time before the first nap of the day. Initially stretching the awake period to two and a half hours is perfect. Let your child nap for as long as they want; this nap may be a little longer than they usually take as they have had a longer awake period before sleeping.

The next awake period should also be made a little longer; adding another 30 minutes is perfect. You don't want the second nap to be too long; the longer this nap is, the later bedtime will be, so you will want to wake your child from this second nap four hours before bedtime. The second nap of the day needs to be just long enough to keep your child going until bedtime. They will need at least four hours of awake time between waking from their second nap and going to sleep at the beginning of the night.

Every third day, push the morning nap a little later, but keep the awake period between naps one and two at three and a half hours. Continue to wake your child as needed from the second nap so you can keep bedtime consistent.

When the first nap of the day has been pushed to around lunchtime, you can drop the second short nap altogether. You may want to move bedtime a little earlier when you do this, but not too early; 30 or 45 minutes early should be perfect. If bedtime is too early, your child may treat the beginning of the night as a nap, sleeping for a few hours and then needing to be up for four hours before sleeping for the rest of the night, which makes for a very late bedtime.

Common Challenges and Solutions

There are a few things that seem to mess with sleep, but luckily, there are uniform ways to deal with these, so it takes the guesswork out of it.

Teething and illness will always disrupt your child's sleep. While your child is uncomfortable and in pain, they are likely to need some extra help through the night. They may struggle to fall asleep and are likely to wake much more often, so you may feel like you've taken several steps backward. Don't worry about creating bad habits—give them the support they need. You can always get back on track when they are more comfortable.

During these times, the best thing to do is be sympathetic and supportive and help your child get the best rest possible. This may mean walking the floor with them, rocking them, or sleeping nearby. When that tooth has broken through the gum or your child is on the mend, you will want to work on getting back to better sleep. The longer your child has had some challenging sleep, the longer it will take them to get back to the normal routine. Treat this sleep disturbance much like a regression, returning to your sleep-training technique if you need to give your child an extra nudge in the right direction.

EXERCISE:
Mindfulness for Self-Compassion

Like parenting, helping your child with their sleep can be hard work. Taking a self-compassion break is an opportunity for you to check in with yourself. Even a few minutes of self-compassion can be a much-needed time-out from negative self-talk.

It would be ideal to sit somewhere quiet, calm, and relaxing for a few minutes before you begin the exercise, but that's not always possible when you are in the thick of it. If you can get away for a minute or two, then do so. Go ahead and put your child into their crib so you can take a breather in another room to do this exercise. Even if your child is upset, they are safe, and this will only take a couple of minutes.

1. Acknowledge and accept the moment of suffering: "I'm so tired. I feel so overwhelmed by the crying."

2. Acknowledge that you are not the first parent to feel this way: "I'm not the first parent to feel this way. Every parent has felt the same feelings."

3. Offer yourself compassion and kindness: "May I have the compassion I need to get through the day."

4. Take a deep breath in through your nose and out through your mouth, and then return to your baby and continue the process.

When Sleep Regression Hits . . .

Regressions are a normal part of sleep development and happen at regular intervals. A regression can make you feel like all the hard work you've put into working on your child's sleep is wasted, but I assure you it's not. Regressions happen at specific ages, and you can get sleep back on track as quickly as possible by sticking closely and consistently to your routines. Here is an overview of the sleep regressions your child will go through:

○ **The 4-month regression:** This regression happens when your child moves from infant sleep cycles to adult sleep cycles.

○ **The 9-month regression:** This is a big regression. A lot is happening with your child's physical development; they are now learning to move around, crawl, pull up to furniture and walk around holding on to it, and even walk. Then comes a period of separation anxiety where your child doesn't want you out of their sight. This may mean they have a tougher time falling asleep alone and need more help when they naturally wake during the night.

○ **The 12-month regression:** The 12-month regression is not as challenging as the 9-month regression. This regression is a little blip and should only last around a week.

○ **The 18-month regression:** This regression can feel more challenging since you are not dealing with a baby anymore; you are working with a highly opinionated toddler who knows what they want and what they don't want. This regression impacts naps more than night sleep.

○ **The 24-month regression:** Much like the 18-month regression, this one can be challenging. This regression has more of an impact on the beginning of the night, and your child may procrastinate when it comes to falling asleep.

You want to get over whichever regression your child is going through as quickly as possible. The good news is that regressions don't last forever. Some regressions are certainly more challenging than others, but they all come to an end.

During a regression, your child is likely to need more help getting to sleep and maybe more help getting back to sleep when they wake throughout the night. Always try to have your child fall asleep according to their usual routine and add more help if you need to. That may require you to leave the room after you have put them to bed. If they are quite upset—that is, crying urgently, not just being noisy and chatting away—you can return to the bedroom and offer some assistance. You can start by talking soothingly to them. If that doesn't work, you can add a little more help. Maybe a tummy rub will suffice. You can sit next to the bed, pick them up for a short while, and rock them for a few moments. Gradually adding this help means you are giving your child the support they need rather than overhelping.

Remain consistent with your routines while going through a regression. Though you may not feel that your routines are helping your child to sleep, the consistency of them is relaxing and will help your child feel more secure.

You should be back on track fairly quickly with all sleep regressions apart from the nine-month sleep regression. This regression can be far more challenging as it can last for a couple of months. During the nine-month sleep regression, try to remain as consistent as you can.

What If I Feel Judged for Sleep Training My Baby?

You know your child better than anyone else on the planet; you know what's right for your family. That may be vastly different from how your neighbor or best friend parents, and that's okay. Feel confident in your decision to sleep train. You've researched the different techniques, you've chosen a method that would work for your family, and you've persisted. Your child is now sleeping more independently. There's no need to feel ashamed that your family is getting some better sleep. Look at the results of sleep training: How much better do you feel now that you are getting a better night's sleep? What differences do you see in your child? Your family is now well rested, and life is easier when you are well rested. Continue to do what's best for your family, no matter what anyone says. You're the expert in them.

Whatever You Do, Be Consistent

One thing I have realized after working with families for more than 20 years is that when life becomes inconsistent, sleep suffers. You've put a lot of your energy into helping your child become a more independent sleeper, and I know you want them to continue being an independent sleeper. I'm not saying you can't deviate from your child's routines at all, but you don't want those deviations to become your new normal. Remaining consistent will mean your child is sleeping consistently. If the routine become irregular, sleep will become irregular.

How do you keep things consistent when life gets in the way? Protect sleep the best you can. If you have a late night, make sure your child has the opportunity to catch up on a little of the missed sleep the following day. They may not sleep in later in the morning, but they will probably want their nap a little earlier, and it may also be a slightly longer nap than usual. Allow them to catch up on the missed sleep, and get back to your regular routines as soon as you can. The sooner you do so, the sooner you'll be back to more consistent sleep.

Trust Yourself and the Process

Don't underestimate your instincts; you know your child better than anyone. Definitely better than random people at the supermarket who are full of parenting advice, and certainly better than the internet. Trust your instinct when it comes to your family. What works for others may not work for you.

Sleep training can feel like a long, drawn-out process, and because you don't see results instantly, you may wonder if you are doing the right thing and question the method. Try not to worry; remember, this will take time. Trust the process. Look for progress, not perfection. You'll quickly be able to see the small steps of progress you are making, and each of those is a step in the right direction.

How to Parent Through the Noise

When you become a parent, you become a magnet for advice. It doesn't matter if you ask for it or not; everyone has an opinion. You may feel like you are being bombarded with what I'm sure is well-meaning input. Early on, you'll gravitate toward specific sources for advice and support; this may be a website, a book, a family member, or even a friend. Stick to these sources throughout your parenting journey if they continue to work for you, but also be aware that you may want to turn to other sources as your child grows—and that's perfectly acceptable.

Do your own research on any choices you need to make concerning your child. You can listen to well-meaning advice if you choose to, but that doesn't mean you have to take it. Learn from your research and by asking questions of your child's pediatrician and other parents who are in a similar situation as yours or have already gone through it. Then make whatever decision you need to make—from your gut. When you make informed, confident decisions, it is easier to block out the noise and, if you wish, share your reasons for making the choices you have.

How to Explain Sleep Training to Skeptics

Maybe your friends or family think you didn't start sleep training early enough, used the wrong technique, started too soon, etc. Remember, everyone is an expert in *their* own child. What works for your child may not work for another, and vice versa: What works for other families may not work for your family. If people are interested in how you worked with your child to help them get better sleep and you don't mind engaging them in the discussion, explain everything you did: You researched the different sleep-training techniques and found one that would work well for your child's unique temperament and slowly made changes to their sleep.

Honesty is the best policy! Don't feel that you have to agree or pretend to agree to please somebody else, regardless of who they are to you. Listen to everything they have to say and let them finish (no butting in!) before sharing your experience. This will help them feel respected and valued. You're not trying to change their mind when it comes to sleep training; you're just letting them know what worked for you and your family.

Conclusion

As you work through different scenarios that affect your child's sleep, you will feel more comfortable making the adjustments you need to make and you'll find it easier to get back on track. The first time you navigate through these unusual situations, it can feel uncomfortable, as if sleep will never settle again, but it will. I promise.

Chapter 6

Check In with Yourself

BECOMING A PARENT IS NOT EASY, PREGNANCY and childbirth are exhausting, and you're then sent home with a little human being who isn't able to do anything for themselves. You are recovering while trying to get to know this amazing little person. Your hormones are all over the place, and you're dealing with a lack of sleep and even sleep deprivation. Emphasis is often on your little one, and of course, it should be, but let's not forget you. You are equally as important as your little one and need just as much care. If you are running on empty, you have nothing to give to those you are caring for. In this chapter, we'll take a look at some ways to help you adapt to the changes you and your family are going through.

Acknowledge You Are Also Going Through Big Changes

Parenting is hard; just when you are beginning to feel settled, things change. That shift might be a normal developmental stage your child is going through or when you start sleep training. Change makes us feel unsettled, disorientated, and untethered. Even though you may not have been content with how your child was sleeping, at least you knew what to expect; even if that wasn't perfect, it was predictable. Until your child has settled into their new normal of better sleep, you may feel some anxiety and resistance to the changes you are making. When sleep training, sleep may become a little trickier before it gets easier, and that's not always easy. It's okay to feel unsettled.

You have gone through so many changes since becoming a parent; you can't take them all in your stride and love each one. If change is making you feel a little uncomfortable, remind yourself of your sleep goals. When you can look at the end result, it makes the change easier to manage. It's okay not to love each stage and all the changes your family is going through. I didn't enjoy sleepless nights, and even though well-meaning friends and family told me I would miss them one day, I have yet to miss them well over a decade since they stopped.

Check In with Your Co-Parent or Support System

Check in with your partner or support system each day if you can. Making it part of your daily routine will soon become a new daily habit. This check-in gives you both a little time to share parts of your day as well as your feelings. Share both the good and the challenging parts of your day. Start with the good: What went well today? It could be that you got the baby to nap in the crib, you were able to get outside and take a walk, or you showered. It doesn't needs to be a big, momentous thing. Small things are perfect. What was challenging today? That could be a cranky baby, teething pain that seemed to be bothering your child, or you weren't able to take a shower.

Sharing the good and the bad lets your partner know a little more about your day and how you are feeling; it also helps you process your day. Remember also to give your partner a chance to share about their day. This is a time for both of you to share and listen. You may want to schedule this check-in when you meet up with your partner at the end of the day, but anytime you both agree on works.

If you don't have the support of a co-parent at home, make the most of technology by texting, e-mailing, or calling your co-parent, a friend, or relative in your support system. You may even find support online in parenting support groups. If you don't feel you have anyone to check in with, don't be afraid to reach out for support.

Be Honest with Yourself

I bet when you are asked, "How are you?" you automatically answer that you're fine. I know I do. How would it feel if you were honest or actually elaborated on how you are really feeling? As a new parent, try to be honest when you are asked how things are going. Think about it for a second before you answer.

When you're honest with others, you're also being honest with yourself. If there's a universal fact we all know about parenting, it's that you don't really stop much and you're always on the go. Whether you're playing games, making meals, cleaning up a mess (over and over again!), or wiping tears away, life is undoubtedly fast-paced when you've got young children. So take the time to be honest with yourself. How are you really feeling? You may not initially know how you feel, so let that question sit with you for a while. The following exercise guides you through a little self-check; you can do this every day or even just once a week.

The Changing Face of Self-Care

For all the reasons mentioned, it's important to squeeze in time for self-care as often as possible. With that said, your self-care activities do need to be realistic for your circumstances. In the past, you may have gone on a spa retreat and had a luxurious weekend of self-care, but that's just not possible right now. Think about how you can nourish your soul in other ways. No, you can't swing a whole weekend away, but can you get away for an hour a few times a week to go to the yoga studio or gym? Can you take a luxurious bath when your partner is on childcare duty? Can you ask a family member or friend to watch the baby while you read a chapter of a novel? Keep in mind that your idea of realistic soul-nourishing self-care will continue to change as your child grows. Your self-care activities won't look like they did before you started your family, and they won't always look like they do now. Get creative with your idea of self-care and carve out as much time as you can.

EXERCISE:
How Are You Feeling?

Take the time to be honest with yourself. Check in with yourself at least once a week, though daily is fine if that works for you. Find a comfortable place to sit and have a pen and paper handy. Then follow these steps:

1. Take a few breaths in through your nose and out through your mouth. Now ask yourself, "How am I really feeling?" You may not initially be able to answer this question, so let it sit with you for a few moments.

2. After a few moments, make a list of everything you are feeling, understanding that you may feel conflicted. For example, you may feel happy *and* sad, overwhelmed *and* underwhelmed, or nervous *and* relaxed, or any other number or combination of feelings. It's okay to have conflicting feelings.

3. Now ask yourself, "What's making me feel this way?" It won't just be one thing; it will be many things. You can write these things down, too, or just answer them for yourself.

4. Decide if you need to address these feelings. If so, think about how you will address them. For example, do you need more rest or some self-care time? Do you need to check in with your doctor? Do you need to have a heartfelt talk with your partner?

5. If you need to address your feelings, do so at your earliest opportunity or make arrangements with someone to help you to create an opportunity.

Prioritize Self-Care

It might be hard to find time for self-care among the chaos of every-day life, but you *absolutely* should. The well-known saying, "You can't pour from an empty cup," is true. You need to have filled up your cup to have any resources available to give to others, including your children. That's why I think the words "selfish" and "self-care" shouldn't be allowed in the same sentence! And when you're sleep deprived, too? Well, that makes self-care even more important.

Short on sleep? Take a nap. It's the old cliché—sleep when your baby sleeps—but it works, and I can almost guarantee you'll feel better afterward. Oh, and treat yourself to an early night, too!

Hobbies don't have to go out of the window when you have a young child. Naturally, you're going to have less time available to pursue your pre-baby hobbies, but you must have something to concentrate on for yourself. Whether it's crafty activities like knitting, exercise-related such as aerial hoop or yoga, or something completely different, there's something for everyone, which inevitably means there's something for you. You need to figure out what makes you happy!

Looking after yourself can fall down your list of priorities pretty quickly when you're looking after a little one, so why not give yourself a confidence boost by getting a haircut and/or having a manicure. It doesn't have to be much. If you wear makeup, simply applying some lipstick can be enough to make you feel more human again.

A healthy dose of escapism could do you a world of good, so pop into your local library or bookshop and find a new novel to get lost in. Of course, you can also choose a book and have it delivered with a simple click. Not much of a bookworm? I've got one word for you—Netflix.

Adult interaction? Not overrated! If you spend all day with your child, make sure you're squeezing in some adult conversation. Text or call family and friends, and go places where you can meet and chat with other adults.

Ask for Help

Remember when your baby was born? All the friends and family who asked you to let them know if you need anything? They meant it; they weren't just saying it to be polite. Don't be afraid to reach out if you need a little help. It's not so easy to ask for help, but people do want to help you, I promise.

If someone asks if you need anything, take them up on the offer of support. Maybe you need someone to hold the baby while you grab a quick shower or even pick up some groceries for you. Your friends and family want to support you, and they will be delighted if you reach out. Asking for help doesn't mean you're not coping; we all need help from time to time. When you receive some much-needed help, you'll feel more positive and less stressed. That's better for you and your family overall.

About Postpartum Depression

Up to 80 percent of new mothers experience the baby blues within the first few weeks after their baby has been born. The baby blues usually go away on their own. Between 10 and 15 percent of new mothers suffer from postpartum depression (PPD). If you have PPD, you may have a feeling that something is not quite right. You may be experiencing any of the following:

○ Anger

○ Changes in appetite

○ Difficulty concentrating

○ Difficulty falling asleep or back asleep

○ Feeling anxious

○ Feeling irritable

○ Feeling guilt, sadness, helplessness, or other "negative" feelings

○ Tearfulness and crying

Check in with your doctor if you are struggling with or think you are struggling with any of these symptoms. Please don't feel that you are failing; you're not. What you are doing is putting your and your family's needs first. Your doctor can help you decide on the best course of action. Depression is nothing to be ashamed of. Talk with your partner, a close friend, or a family member about how you are feeling. Getting support not only from your doctor, but from your family and friends can help set you on the path to feeling better.

Dealing with Loneliness

I meet so many families who tell me that they've found their parenting journey tough so far and that the feeling of loneliness has come as something of a surprise. The problem may be that many new parents are fooled into thinking that the whole business of having a baby should be cherished and enjoyed, no matter what. But that is just impossible. There's no way we can all find joy in every minute of our lives, but for some reason, we strive to do just that. Social-media pressures, television commercials, and even parenting manuals seem to imply that life as a new parent should be precious and filled with love, happiness, and connection. When the reverse is true, we find it hard to admit.

When you're at home with a new baby and everyone else is at work, it really can be a lonely time. Even at the best of times, you may struggle with not feeling sociable. Now you're staying close to home during sleep training and you are feeling tired and sleep deprived, making the struggle even more difficult. You may feel even more isolated, and the days can seem to stretch on and on.

That's okay. Once you admit that you're feeling lonely, the next step is to make some changes to your daily routine so that you can turn things around. Take a look at where you can make changes. Sometimes being tied to a strict routine can become isolating if you don't allow for spontaneous events or outings now and then. Allow time for flexibility and try to go with the flow a little more. If there are parent groups you can attend, make arrangements to attend one and see how it goes. Take someone along with you for moral support if you can. You can also reach out in online groups and forums. Sometimes the best friendships can be found at the other end of a keyboard.

Set Boundaries with Friends and Family

It's wonderful having friends and family visit, but sometimes they can outstay their welcome. Don't be afraid to set rules with your guests before they come around. Some of my favorites are to let them know how long they are welcome in your home. Would an hour be okay? Would you like them gone before you start your bedtime routine? Don't be afraid to let them know what works best for you when you're discussing their visit. Explaining the reason is helpful. They may not know that your bedtime routine takes nearly an hour, and you don't want to leave them alone while you are helping your child get to sleep. They don't know that all you can cope with that day is an hour if you don't tell them. You don't need to be confrontational. You can say, "I would love it if you came to visit us. We'd love to see you for an hour at 2:00 p.m. I do have something at 3:15 p.m., so an hour's visit would be perfect."

I am also a big fan of having friends and family help out when they visit. Could they do the dishes? Bring something for dinner? Let them know in advance that you would like them to help you out. When you send the group e-mail to all your friends and family with those first pictures of your little one, let them know that they are welcome to arrange a time to visit with you and the baby. Tell them that you'd certainly love to see them, but that you will not be available for unplanned visits. Also, let them know that you would like them to help out in some way during their scheduled visit. Give them some suggestions, and thank them for being so considerate.

REAL-LIFE STORY

Julie contacted me many years ago in tears. Her eight-month-old son, Daniel, had never been a great sleeper; he needed a lot of help initially falling asleep for his naps and at bedtime, and also needed lots of help getting back to sleep. Daniel was waking at least eight times a night. Helping Daniel to sleep and back to sleep took lots of feeding, rocking, and patience.

Julie was desperate for some sleep. Her pediatrician suggested that Julie let Daniel cry it out and learn to self-soothe. Julie wasn't sure if it would work for Daniel, who had an intense temperament. His cry would become very urgent very quickly, and he would need a lot of support soothing. One night, after trying the technique for eight hours, Julie gave up; Daniel was nowhere near falling asleep.

Julie called me the following morning; she was upset that she had tried a technique she didn't think would work. We worked together, using a much gentler sleep-training technique that Julie was much more comfortable with. With Julie's help, Daniel learned the skills to get himself to sleep and started sleeping for much longer stretches.

EXERCISE:
Three-Minute Relaxation Meditation

Three minutes is all you need to get the benefits of a calmer mind and body. Follow this routine:

1. Find a quiet spot if you can (or use headphones), and sit or lie in a comfortable position.

2. Close your eyes and take a long, deep breath in through your nose and out through your mouth. Continue to breathe in and out.

3. As you breathe, focus on your toes. Wiggle them around a little.

4. Continuing to breathe, move your feet in a circular motion, loosening your ankles. Focus on your calves and knees, and allow them to relax.

5. Turn your attention to your thighs. Relax those large muscles, and then move your focus to your pelvis. Allow that area to relax, too.

6. Remember to keep breathing. As you breathe out, feel your stomach muscles relax, and release any tension in your back. Start with your lower back and work your way up to your shoulders. Drop your shoulders slightly.

7. Open your mouth slightly, releasing tension from your jaw. Relax your eyes and forehead. Let your face go slack.

8. Continue to breathe in and out for another 30 seconds or more.

9. Slowly open your eyes. End your meditation with another deep inhalation and exhalation. You're now ready to carry on with your day.

Figure Out What Works Best for Your Family

Before you brought your baby home, did you think about what kind of parents you will be or what your parenting style is? You may not know the answer to those questions, and your views and opinions will likely change as your child ages. It's okay to change your mind; in fact, it's healthy to learn and adapt. When I was pregnant with my eldest daughter, I was convinced she would never use a pacifier so we didn't have one in our home. That was until she was around four days old. At that point, I realized she would benefit from having a pacifier—that we would *all* benefit from her having a pacifier. I sent my husband out to buy every brand of pacifier because I didn't know which one she would like, and she used a pacifier for longer than I care to admit here.

There's nothing wrong with changing your mind; you'll find what works for your family and, when you find something that works for you all, stick with it (as long as it's safe). But what do we do if we're faced with different parenting styles within one family? If you're parenting with different styles, you're going to need to communicate effectively with your partner. It's not okay to tell your partner that you don't agree and that's that. By being open and communicating effectively, you're better able to explain why you believe your approach works and why you prefer it as opposed to your partner's approach. It can be hard, but you need to be respectful of each other's thoughts and feelings, and try to understand each other's motives and approaches as best you can.

It's not impossible to parent with different styles, but it can present problems from time to time. There are so many ways to ensure your child's needs are being met and that you're both having your say on what's best. Being open, honest, and willing to respect each other's feelings is essential.

Follow Your Heart

As I mentioned earlier, you are probably being bombarded with advice from your family and friends as well as the internet; suddenly, everyone's a parenting expert and will probably be more than happy to share their advice. The information you have received may not sit well with you if the thought of implementing the advice makes you feel uncomfortable or it just seems off. That means it's not right for you or your child. I don't recommend you follow such advice. If you do, you'll make a half-hearted attempt, give up sooner, and feel that you should have followed your heart to begin with. Save yourself the time and energy by following your heart in the first place.

If you follow your instincts, you can't go wrong. So pick up your baby when you want to and lay them down when you want to. If something doesn't feel right to you, then don't do it. As long as you and your family are happy and well rested, then all is good.

Conclusion

Your emotional well-being and your health are essential and just as important as your baby's. Make your health, well-being, and rest a priority. Remember, you can't pour from an empty cup. Make sure you take time to look after yourself and don't feel guilty about enjoying some self-care. In doing so, your family will greatly benefit.

Chapter 7

What to Do When . . .

I CAN'T SAY THIS ENOUGH: YOU'RE THE EXPERT ON your baby and your family. Every baby's development is unique to their experience, so even with all this new information at hand, you might hit a few bumps on the road to peaceful sleep for your baby and yourself. Luckily, I know from years of helping families sleep better that many of these are common obstacles, so I've had plenty of opportunity to help parents tackle them. The following are frequently asked questions I encounter. I hope my answers will help you more smoothly navigate your way to better sleep.

I'm too anxious to leave my baby at night. I check on them every 15 minutes. What if something goes wrong while they are sleeping alone in their crib?

If you are feeling anxious, why not room share with your little one? Bring their crib or bassinet into your room, or make a bed up for yourself in the nursery. That way, you can be near your child while they're sleeping. The American Academy of Pediatrics suggests room sharing for the first 6 to 12 months, as it is safe and actually reduces the risk of SIDS. If the anxiety is crippling, make sure you talk with your doctor about how you are feeling; they will be able to help you. Severe anxiety may be a sign of postpartum depression (see page 119) or postpartum anxiety.

I'm going back to work soon, and I'm struggling to figure out how to keep my baby on a routine when I'm not home all day.

Have some practice mornings before you start back at work. You'll be able to figure out how long you need to get ready in the morning. If you prepare as much as you can the night before, you can streamline your morning routine a little. In the morning, you can get your child up from bed, give them a quick feed, and leave the house on time.

Ask your childcare provider to follow your daily routine. Most childcare providers will follow the schedule you set until they reach about 12 months of age. Let your provider know what time they will need to help your child to sleep for the first nap when you drop them off in the morning.

Stick to the same daily schedule even when you are not working. I know the idea of sleeping in on a Saturday morning sounds blissful, but the more consistent your child's daily schedule is, the easier time they will have on the mornings you need to be up early. The consistent start to the day will also help their bedtime remain consistent. A late start to the day will lead to late naps and a late bedtime, causing a later start the following day. This can cause bedtime to gradually shift later and later, and your child is likely to miss out on sleep.

I'm trying to sleep train more than one child. Help!
Don't feel that you need to train all your children at the same time. Often, it's much easier to start sleep training the child who has a more intense temperament. The more intense child will have much less wiggle room when it comes to their routines. They won't be able to handle being overtired as easily as a child who is more laid-back and easygoing. Sleep training will take a little more planning, and you can only be in one place at one time. Having someone help you can also make a big difference.

You can, of course, sleep train multiples together. You may feel a little stretched since you can only help one child at a time. With twins or more, an extra pair of hands may be what you need to succeed. Don't worry about not being able to have separate rooms for your multiples to sleep in if you are sleep training them at the same time; they will need to get used to sleeping through each other's noises.

My older child doesn't understand why their newborn sibling needs so much sleep. They throw a tantrum every time I try to put the baby down.
This must be very frustrating. I remember something similar happening to my older daughter when my youngest daughter was born. To remedy this, I kept my older daughter's favorite toys in a box and would only get this box out when I really needed it, mainly during my younger daughter's sleep times and feed times. As she could only have those toys at set times, she was more likely to want to play with them. Another suggestion is to have your toddler involved in the nap and bedtime routine; this routine can take place in your bedroom. Let your toddler choose the books to read, choose the songs to sing to the baby, etc. Having your older child as involved as possible in the routine will help them be a little less jealous of their new sibling.

I really want to try co-sleeping/bed sharing with my baby. Is there a way to make sleep training work if the baby is with me in my bed?

You certainly can sleep train if you are safely bed sharing (see page 76). It is trickier, but it is possible. First, you will want to make sure that your sleep space is safe. You won't be able to leave your child alone in the bed for safety reasons, so really think long and hard about whether sharing a bed is best for you. Maybe having your child sleep on a separate surface next to your bed would be a good fit for your family. If you do want to share a bed with your child and you would like to sleep train, you will want to use one of the gentler sleep-training techniques, such as the Michi method, Pat-the-Baby, or Tippy-Toe-Out (though you will not be physically leaving the room). Families may find night feeds a little trickier when bed sharing, so try to be very consistent and strict with yourself and how you time night feeds.

When can I move my child from a crib to a toddler bed?

I have found it easier to move a child from their crib to a bed before two years old or after three years old. A two-year-old can be very impulsive, and they may struggle to remain in bed. They'll get out of bed simply because they can, and this can happen many times a night—many, many times a night.

When you do transition your child to a toddler bed, you will want to make sure the bedroom has been childproofed. Attach heavy furniture to the wall, cover outlets, and make sure window blind and electrical cords are out of the way. Your child will be able to get up out of bed and will be free to roam around their bedroom while you are sleeping. Don't start a habit you do not want to continue long term. I often hear from parents that their child kept jumping out of their toddler bed when they made the switch, so they stayed in the room with their child until they fell asleep. That way, they could easily prevent them from getting out of bed. This may seem like a good fix, but your child will now expect that treatment every night and when they naturally wake during the night.

Don't start doing something that can bite you on the bum in the future. If your child repeatedly jumps out of bed, wait outside their door, which should be open a crack, and as soon as you see your child try to get out of bed, firmly say, "It's time to sleep, stay in bed." (There's no need to shout here.) If they continue to get out of bed, enter the room, take them by the hand, and walk them back to bed. Try to encourage your child to be as independent as possible. They can get into bed and pull their covers up over themselves; that way, they are not relying on you to get them comfortable in bed. Then leave the room. Repeat, repeat, repeat.

Your child may jump out of bed for what feels like a million times, and their bedtime is getting awfully delayed, but stick with it. Keep returning them to bed as needed. You may regret ever transitioning them to a bed, but keep at it. They will finally get it. I promise.

My child will only nap for 20 minutes. How can I lengthen their naps?

Twenty-minute naps are common for children whose brains are overstimulated before they fall asleep. Luckily, there is a quick fix to relax your child's brain a little before beginning their nap routine. Pick your child up from whatever they have been doing about 10 minutes before you are planning to start your nap routine. Walk around the house with them in your arms, looking out of the windows and at pictures on the wall. Walk at a slow, steady pace. This will help relax your child's brain a little more before you begin your nap routine and will help them sleep. You should now be able to avoid the 20-minute wake-ups.

How do I transition my child from the swaddle?

Your child will need to learn how to sleep with much more freedom of movement of their arms, and this can take a little time. If you get started early enough, before your child is rolling from back to front unswaddled, you can gradually make the transition. Start with a nap or at the very beginning of the night. You can always reswaddle them if you need to. If your child is rolling from their back to front when they are unswaddled, you will need to transition them right away. Rolling while swaddled can be dangerous, as your child is unable to push up on their hands when they need to. You may have some tough days or nights as they get used to the new way of sleeping. Things should settle down after three or four days or nights.

When should I get my child on a daily schedule?

I wouldn't even attempt to get onto a daily schedule until your child is 12 weeks old. Go from their due date, not their birth date, as sleep develops at a set pace. Trying to get onto a routine before you are ready can be very frustrating for both you and your child.

When can I introduce a bedtime routine?

You can add a bedtime routine at any age. I like to introduce one at around 12 weeks.

My eight-month-old wakes too early in the morning (5:00 a.m.). How can I help them sleep later in the morning?

Early wake-ups are tough! Children may wake early in the morning for a couple of reasons: Their bedtime is too early, they're getting too much daytime sleep, or they may just be an early riser. Take a look at when your child is going to bed at night. If they are going to sleep at 6:00 p.m., a 5:00 a.m. wake-up is reasonable. You can try slowly pushing their bedtime a little later, for example, 10 minutes later every fourth night. Mornings can take a while to catch up (waiting two weeks to see a later start to the day is not unusual), so don't rush; you don't want your child to miss out on too much sleep.

A child who is sleeping too much during the day may also start their day a little too early. Take a look at the daily routine examples in chapter 3 to see how long your child should roughly be sleeping each day. Remember, every child is different and has unique sleep needs. Some children are just early risers—sorry! There may not be anything you can do to change the time they are up and ready to go in the morning. If you have an early riser, remember it won't always be this way. They will become teenagers who you won't be able to drag out of bed in the morning, and you will have great pleasure waking them up early for school.

When can I give my child a pillow?
Some families wait until their child has moved into a bed before introducing them to a pillow. You can happily add a pillow from around 18 months old. You will want to make sure that the pillow is not too thick. Lots of companies make small, thin pillows just for toddlers.

My 17-month-old is fighting their second nap. Are they ready for one nap a day?
Children usually go down to one nap per day sometime between 12 and 18 months; the average age is 15 months. Some signs your child is ready to transition to one nap are: They struggle to fall asleep for either nap, but more likely the second nap of the day; they have a harder time falling asleep at the beginning of the night; and they are beginning to wake up earlier in the morning. The best way to transition is to do it gradually.

Make the morning nap about 30 minutes later and let them nap as long as they want. Lengthen the time between the first and second nap by 30 minutes, but make sure the second nap is just long enough to keep your child going until bedtime. That may mean waking them from this nap before they are ready. If they nap as long as they want, bedtime will be very late. Every fourth day, make the first nap later, which will, in turn, push the second nap later. Make sure you continue to monitor the duration of the second nap. As the first nap reaches lunchtime, you'll have no time for the second nap, and you will have successfully transitioned to one nap a day.

I no longer swaddle my child. What should my child wear to sleep?
I recommend placing children in a sleep sack after they have transitioned from the swaddle. A sleep sack will keep your child warm; it is

essentially a wearable blanket. Loose blankets in the crib can be very dangerous: Your child won't be able to kick off these covers and they present a suffocation risk. Another reason I love sleep sacks is that they can prevent a toddler from climbing out of the crib; there just isn't enough room in a sleep sack for them to reach their leg up to the top of the rail and climb out.

How much sleep should my child be getting at night?

The amount of sleep your child needs depends on their age. Use the following table, which is based on recommendations from the National Sleep Foundation, to guide you. Remember, every child will have an ideal amount of necessary sleep that is unique to them.

AGE	RECOMMENDED HOURS OF SLEEP
0 to 3 months	14 to 17 hours per 24 hours
4 to 11 months	12 to 15 hours per 24 hours (two or three naps a day)
1 to 2 years	11 to 14 hours per 24 hours (one or two naps a day)
3 to 5 years	10 to 13 hours per 24 hours (one nap a day)
6 to 13 years	9 to 11 hours per 24 hours

Why will my baby sleep for the nanny, but not for me?

It's not unusual for children to behave very differently for different caretakers; you may even notice that your child treats you and your partner differently. Your child feels completely themselves when they are with you; they like you, and they don't want to miss out on a second of being with you. Take it as a compliment. But that doesn't mean you can't help them sleep a little easier. Sleep training will help them not only learn the skills to get to sleep but let them know what you expect of them. Sleep training teaches new skills and helps them learn to use the skills they already have to get themselves to sleep—no matter who is in charge of putting them in their crib.

Are there any supplements that can help my child sleep?

Always talk with your child's pediatrician if you are considering giving your child supplements to help them sleep. **Important:** Do not give your child any substance without their doctor's approval.

My toddler wants to have a snack before bed at night. What foods should I offer?

Foods high in the amino acid tryptophan, which has a calming effect on the brain, are a perfect snack to offer before bedtime. The body converts the amino acid into serotonin, which helps us feel calmer and produces melatonin, which induces sleep. Foods high in tryptophan include whole-grain cereal with milk, oatmeal with milk, yogurt and granola, banana, and almonds. **Important:** Do not offer these foods before your child is ready for them. Always check with your pediatrician before offering new food to your child.

Is there a perfect age to start sleep training?

I don't think there is an ideal age, but there are times that are easier than others. I like to sleep train between six and nine months. This seems to be quite a stable time developmentally. There is a small regression around six months, but it doesn't have enough of an impact to delay sleep training. My second favorite time to sleep train is between 12 and 18 months of age. Again, this is a calmer time developmentally, which makes it a good time for sleep training.

There is always something going on in your child's life that may disrupt sleep, such as teething, developmental stages, illnesses, and travel, to name a few. You don't want to start sleep training if your child is uncomfortable or in pain. You also wouldn't want to get started if you are traveling or another big event is happening soon. Going through a developmental stage can also cause a sleep regression and is not the best time to get started. It may not look like there are many times that are good for sleep training, but luckily most illnesses do not last long, and teeth eventually come in and stop causing discomfort. So anytime you don't have big things happening is a good time to begin sleep training.

I sleep trained my child a few months ago and they were sleeping really well, but then they got sick and began waking up several times each night. How do I get them (and myself) back on track?

It's not unusual for sleep to become more challenging when your child is unwell. We all wake more often when we are sick. When your child is feeling better, you can work on getting back to better sleep. Don't wait until you feel that you have caught up on a little sleep before you get back on track; the longer you wait, the harder it will be. The best way to get your child back on track is to go through your sleep training again, from square one. Don't worry; it won't be as challenging as it was when you first got started. Your child has not forgotten all the skills you taught them; they just need a nudge in the right direction and a reminder to use those skills again. If your child was sick for a week or less, you should be back on track within a night or two. If you were out of good habits for up to two weeks, it might take your child three or four nights to adjust.

My toddler keeps climbing out of their crib in the middle of the night. Now what?

From the top of the crib rail to the floor is a long way, and for their safety, you will want to transition your child to a bed. This could be a toddler bed or a twin bed. First, I suggest placing them into a sleep sack to see if that prevents them from being able to get their leg to the top of the crib rail. If they are jumping up and launching themselves over the rail, a sleep sack won't help. If they are not launching themselves over the rail, the sleep sack may get you a few more months' use out of their crib. If the sleep sack isn't going to work for you, you will need to transition them to a bed. See my answer to "When can I move my child from a crib to a toddler bed?" on page 130.

Resources

**Ask Dr. Sears: The Trusted Resource for
    Parents:** www.askdrsears.com
Postpartum Support International: www.postpartum.net
Rebecca Michi: Children's Sleep Consultant:
    www.childrenssleepconsultant.com
Slumber Academy: www.slumberacademy.com

References

Abdullah, Maryam. "Self-Compassion for Parents." *Greater Good Magazine*, April 17, 2018. Accessed December 11, 2019. greatergood.berkeley.edu/article/item/self_compassion _for_parents.

Franco, P., N. Seret, J. N. Van Hees, S. Scaillet, F. Vermeulen, J. Grosswasser, and A. Kahn. "Decreased Arousals Among Healthy Infants After Short-Term Sleep Deprivation." *Pediatrics* 114, no. 2 (August 2004): 192–197. doi:10.1542/peds.114.2.e192.

Gradisar, Michael, Kate Jackson, Nicola J. Spurrier, Joyce Gibson, Justine Whitham, Anne Sved Williams, Robyn Dolby, and David J. Kennaway. "Behavioral Interventions for Infant Sleep Problems: A Randomized Controlled Trial." *Pediatrics* 137, no. 6 (June 2016). doi.org/10.1542/peds.2015-1486.

National Center for Biotechnology Information. "Pregnancy and Birth: Reflux in Babies," July 2008, March 2018. Accessed December 19, 2019. https://www.ncbi.nlm.nih.gov/books/NBK343315/.

National Sleep Foundation. "How Much Sleep Do Babies and Kids Need?" Accessed December 19, 2019. https://www .sleepfoundation.org/excessive-sleepiness/support/how -much-sleep-do-babies-and-kids-need.

Weinraub, M., R. H. Bender, S. L. Friedman, E. J. Susman, B. Knoke, R. Bradley, R. Houts, and J. Williams. "Patterns of Developmental Change in Infants' Nighttime Sleep Awakenings from 6 Through 36 Months of Age." *Developmental Psychology* 48, no. 6 (November 2012): 1511–28. doi:10.1037/a0027680.

Index

Acknowledgments

I have to start by thanking my amazing husband, Matteo. Your support not only when writing this book but also throughout my business has meant the world to me. You are my biggest cheerleader. I love you.

My amazing daughters, you teach me every day how to be a better person. Keep dreaming big and, remember, don't fall over.

Special thanks to my parents, who have always believed in me and told me always to try my hardest. I try every day.

My brother and his lovely family, I wish we could hang out more. I miss you lots.

The fantastic team at Callisto Media, thank you. I had no idea it took so many people to get a book published. Emily, your support has kept me going in the right direction.

Lucy, your work behind the scenes, keeping me heading in the right direction each day, has been a blessing. Thank you.

Special thanks to Amy. I love working next to you in coffee shops.

Birgit, I love our walks with coffee. Thank you for being a special friend.

To all the hundreds of families who have trusted me to help them get a better night's sleep: thank you, thank you, thank you. I adore working with you all. Helping your family get a better night's sleep gives me so much joy.

About the Author

Rebecca Michi is a children's sleep consultant and founder of Slumber Academy, a membership website that specializes in teaching parents how to sleep train their children gently. She has more than 25 years of experience working with families in many different capacities. She has been specializing in children's sleep for more than a decade. Rebecca speaks at parenting conferences all over North America and often teams up with other parenting experts for workshops and classes. She lives in Seattle, Washington, with her husband, two teenage daughters, and German shepherd.